Woven by Love

&⁊

A Memoir

&⁊

By Angel Tien Le

A life woven by Love Himself is a life that chooses to love again and again,

no matter how much hardship it has endured.

— Angel Tien Le

To my mother,
and to those who love quietly.

Author's Note

This story was stitched from memory.

Some names have been changed. Some scenes have been softened. But the love — the mother who waited with tea, the daughter who searched for light, the quiet faith that rose through every silence — all of that is real.

The white space in this book is intentional. It is not emptiness, but room to breathe — a pause for the heart to linger on a moment before moving on. Life rarely speaks in long, unbroken lines; it comes in fragments, glances, and quiet revelations. I wanted the pages to hold that same rhythm.

I didn't write *Woven by Love* to be brave. I wrote it because I couldn't forget.

I wrote it for my mother, Le. For the women who raised us in rooms that leaked, who sewed when their backs ached, who loved quietly and never asked for recognition.

And I wrote it for you.

Whether you are a daughter, a mother, or simply someone trying to find peace in a noisy world — I hope this book finds you gently. I hope it reminds you that love, when chosen again and again, can hold a life together.

If you find pieces of yourself in these pages, I pray you walk away not with heaviness — but with hope.

Throughout this story, you'll find moments where Tien cries out to "God" — in fear, in silence, in longing.

During her early life, Tien and her family followed the Buddhist faith. At that time, the word "God" expressed the divine presence they honoured through incense, reverence, and quiet prayer — a longing shaped by the traditions of her mother, Le.

Although Tien did not yet know God through Christ, her heart still reached for something greater — and even then, He was already nearby.

I chose to keep the word "God" throughout these early chapters, not to erase the spiritual background of her childhood, but to reflect the deep emotional truth of those moments. When a child prays, even without full understanding, the cry is still sacred. It still reaches heaven.

Tien found God's name later —

but He had been listening the whole time.

Thank you for reading my story.
It is an honour to place it in your hands.

With love,
Angel Tien Le

Table of Contents

Ꝋ

Dedication
Author's Note
Prologue
Characters

Prologue
And the Thread That Led Me Here

§

I didn't set out to write a book. I set out to remember —

to gather the small things that made me who I am:

boiled eggs with salt and pepper, jasmine tea on tired evenings,

the scent of damp clay and sewing thread.

For many years, I believed my story was too quiet to matter.

But God was always writing —

through broken rice, unspoken prayers,

and the voice I found when I stopped needing permission to speak.

This is not a story of triumph.

It is a story of staying.

Of forgiving.

Of beginning again after every rain.

If you are holding this book, I hope it meets you gently.

I hope you find your own thread in these pages —

and follow it home.

Characters

The threads that hold this story together

৯৬

Tien

The daughter.

Quiet and determined. She grows up learning to carry hardship with gentleness and to rise without resentment.

Le

The mother.

A tailor with worn hands and a warrior's heart. Her love is stitched into every bowl of congee and every night spent at the sewing machine.

Minh

The brother.

Kind, steady, and protective. He is Tien's shelter in the storm, her kite-flying companion, and a quiet reminder that she is never alone.

Andrew

The husband.

A man of faith and calm laughter who meets Tien through truth. In his quiet presence, she finds peace and rain-soaked joy.

Lan

The sister-in-law.

Minh's wife, whose coldness and pride cast a quiet shadow over Tien's final school years.

Mrs Dan

Tien's English teacher.

Soft-spoken and kind, she sees more than she says and offers quiet encouragement that Tien never forgets.

Mrs Linh

The librarian.

Soft-spoken and kind. She sees the quiet hunger in Tien and offers knowledge, snacks, and unspoken understanding.

Mila

Tien's loyal childhood dog.

Fiercely protective and quietly constant, Mila offered companionship during some of her loneliest years. His tragic loss marked one of Tien's first encounters with grief that had no answer — only silence, and the love that stays even after goodbye.

Milu

The dog who stayed.

Tien's loyal friend and silent comfort through long nights of study, illness, and recovery.

The Village

Tailoring customers, classmates, teachers, neighbours.

A mix of compassion and cruelty, shaping Tien's journey through whispers, warmth, and quiet acts of grace or harm.

Chapter 1
The Day the Rain Came
And the Light That Was Born in the Dark

෪

May 2025 – Australia

It was raining again.

Not the wild, angry kind — just a steady patter on the rooftop.

Soft like breath, familiar like a song remembered from long ago.

Tien sat at her piano, barefoot, hands resting on the keys but unmoving.

The rain was playing for her today.

Through the open window came the scent of wet soil — grass, leaves, and that hush that always came with Australian autumn.

She closed her eyes.

It reminded her of something.

No — someone.

"You were born on a rainy night," her mother once told her.

"Outside, the world was dark. But inside this house — a new light had come."

1990 – Vietnam

The rain came quietly that night — neither harsh nor shy.

It slipped through the leaves, tapped the roof, and waited outside the door.

In a small house stitched together with palm leaves and gentle prayers, Le held her newborn daughter to her chest.

Her body ached.

Her mind was quiet.

But her arms were strong.

The baby was warm, wrapped in faded cloth, her eyelids fluttering like the world was already whispering stories to her.

Minh, twelve years old, crouched nearby.

He looked at his sister like she was the only good thing he had ever seen.

Their father was already gone again — drifting in and out of presence like love was a door he couldn't stay inside.

But Minh stayed.

"Her name is Tien," Le said, just loud enough for the rain to hear.

"It means heaven."

And in that moment, heaven didn't feel far.

Some mornings, there was no food in the house.

But out the back, Le had raised a single hen.

Every day, the chicken laid one egg.

And every day, Le would boil it gently, slice it in half, and sprinkle just a pinch of salt and pepper on top.

She never touched it. Neither did Minh.

The egg was for Tien — still wobbling on unsteady feet, babbling her favourite word:

"Egggg."

They watched her eat it like it was a feast.

And maybe it was.

Not because of what it cost.

But because of what it meant.

Chapter 2
The Road Out
And the Way to Freedom

&

Tien had just turned one when her father left.

No note.

No goodbye.

Just the sudden, hollow silence that settled in his absence.

Minh knew better than to ask.

He was used to the sound of doors closing behind him.

Le remembered the soft shuffle of his slippers on the floor.

The way the door shut — not slammed, just... finished.

She waited an hour.

Then two.

Minh said nothing. Neither did she.

But from that night on, the hallway no longer held silence.

It held absence.

This time, Le didn't hide her sorrow.

And the world didn't hide its scorn.

Her own family — the ones who once ate at her wedding table — whispered louder now.

"Twice abandoned."

"No luck in her blood."

"What a shame."

Even the small patch of land her mother had given her — a thin strip behind the banana trees — was taken back.

No discussion. Just one bitter word:

"Go."

So, she packed quietly.

Some clothes.

A few tools.

The sewing machine an older sister once gave her.

Tien's milk bottle.

Minh's books.

It didn't take long. They didn't have much.

As they stepped outside — Le holding Tien close to her chest, Minh trailing behind — she heard it:

Laughter.

Not strangers.

Family.

Sharper, because it came from the ones who once loved her.

"Let her go. She's nothing but bad luck."

"Two children. No husband. She thinks she's still one of us?"

Minh stared at the road, fists clenched, jaw tight.

But the tears came anyway — slow, quiet.

Le's fell too. She didn't wipe them.

She let them soak into Tien's blanket, one by one,

as her cheek rested against her baby's hair.

Each step away was a step through shame.

And one step closer to freedom.

Chapter 3
The Roof Beneath the Storm
And the Shelter Built by Grace

The laughter of kin echoed behind her —

not with warmth, but with mockery.

Cast out again, this time with a child in her arms,

Tien's mother stood beneath the rain,

her heart shattered, her pockets holding only the last trace of dignity
— a few crumpled notes.

With nowhere to go, she paused under a stranger's awning.

There, in the downpour, a kind woman noticed her tears and asked gently,

"What happened?"

Le told her. Not everything. Just enough.

The woman hesitated, then whispered about a house.

Cheap. Too cheap.

No one wanted it — not because of the walls,

but the whispers: mafia-run, unsafe, unlucky.

It was all Le could afford.

She bought it with everything she had,

knowing she wasn't buying comfort — only a fragile chance to begin again.

The house barely stood.

But hope never asked for grandeur.

Tien's seventh uncle, quiet and kind, came to help.

With calloused hands, he laid bricks and dreams side by side.

One of Le's tailoring clients, moved by her story, chopped down her own trees

so the timber could become the bones of Tien's new home.

Inside that half-built shelter,

two-year-old Tien lay sleeping in her mother's arms.

Unaware of the storm.

Unaware of the pain.

She didn't know the roof above them was born from sacrifice —

that every wall was nailed with tears and stitched with silent prayers.

But maybe that's what childhood is meant to be:

safe in the arms of a mother who bears the world,

so her child doesn't have to.

12

Chapter 4
The Little House and the Big Knife
And the Stitching of Fear and Hope

Tien grew up in a violent neighbourhood,

where safety meant silence,

and Le worked tirelessly through the night.

Amid fear and exhaustion, she clung to one fragile hope:

to earn enough to move them somewhere safe.

Life settled into a kind of quiet resistance.

They lived tucked away in their fragile little house,

where the cost of peace was never speaking up.

Even when neighbours tied pigs outside their door,

and the stench of dung soaked into everything,

they stayed quiet.

Complaints could bring knives.

And in that part of town, knives didn't just threaten —

they cut.

Some nights, chaos spilled into the streets —

feet pounding, metal flashing, voices shattering the dark.

Tien would cling to Le,

both frozen in a silence deeper than fear.

Sometimes bodies slammed into their walls,

making the thin timber shudder.

Once, a blade even sliced through the palm roof

and tore down part of the wall.

"Don't worry, the house will survive," Le whispered, holding her tightly.

"We don't need to fix anything."

Tien never saw her cry.

But she felt the tremble in her arms —

the slight, unspoken quake when the knife met the wood.

"Will they pay us if they break our house, Mum?" she asked once.

"No, dear," Le replied softly, pulling her closer.

"And don't ask that question to anyone."

Most nights, Tien went to bed alone.

Le worked late, sewing under a weak bulb that buzzed like a tired wasp.

Often, Tien would wake to find her still hunched at the machine,

hands moving in a trance between fabric and thread.

But before she sat down to work each night,

Le would slip a knife under her pillow.

"Just in case," she told Tien,

in the same tone she used when reminding her to wear a hat going out.

To Tien, that knife was a kind of protection —

but it was also terrifying.

It meant the danger was close enough to reach them in sleep.

It meant her mother was afraid, too.

Eventually, Tien learned her mother worked twenty — sometimes twenty-two — hours a day.

One night, she sat up and whispered,

"Mum, come to sleep."

"I need to earn money," Le said gently, without looking up.

"When we have enough, we'll buy a house far from here.

Somewhere quiet. Somewhere safe."

And so, the needle kept moving,

and the dream stayed alive — stitched into every seam.

But there were moments of light, too.

Tien's father visited once, unexpectedly.

He brought English books, even though she hadn't started school.

Minh sat with her, teaching her ABCs,

and soon she was reading — blending words like puzzle pieces.

"She doesn't need kindergarten," Minh told Le.

"Put her straight into Year One."

And so they did — one year ahead of the legal age.

Later, her father returned with science books.

Big, glossy pages filled with planets, electricity, strange inventions.

"For Tien to read later," he said.

Tien didn't know it then, but those books would shape the way she saw the world — with wonder, precision, and curiosity.

Her mother once said, "If it wasn't for your dad, I wouldn't even know what books to buy. He's an educated man — I left school early."

But the moment that struck deepest came during a visit to the city.

They were walking through a mall, holding hands,

when Tien saw a toy shop filled with colour and light.

And standing inside — smiling, laughing — was her father.

Beside him, a well-dressed woman.

His new wife.

Their toy shop.

Tien stared, unsure whether to run or wave.

The woman noticed them. Perhaps out of kindness.

She stepped outside, knelt to Tien's level,

and placed something small in her hands:

A toy keyboard.

She had never touched an instrument before.

Never seen one up close.

But when her fingers pressed the plastic keys and sound rose,

something stirred.

A seed was planted.

When they returned home, Le received a call from Tien's father.

His voice was cold and clipped:

"Don't bring Tien here again.

I don't want to ruin the happiness of my family."

Tien didn't fully understand the words.

But she saw the way Le's lips tightened,

felt the tears that welled in both their eyes.

Rejection doesn't always shout.

Sometimes it just closes a door quietly —

and walks away.

But even closed doors can't stop a child from dreaming.

Especially a child who had already heard the sound of keys

and found joy inside a science book.

22

Chapter 5
The Strongest Silence
And the Egg That Said Everything

๛

Year One was supposed to be about colours and counting, recess and laughter.

But for Tien, it began with silence — and pain.

One of the girls in her class had overheard her own mother say,

"That Tien has the best hair in the class."

What could've been a compliment turned into something sharp.

Envy, in the hands of children, takes strange shapes.

From then on, that girl — and two others — began to torment her.

They pulled her hair. Pressed her head to the wooden table.

And when she flinched or protested, they slapped her — again and again.

"Don't cry," they hissed.

"Don't make a sound. Or we'll hit you more."

Tien learned to swallow the sting and blink back tears.

Her small fists clenched beneath the desk —

not in anger,

but to keep herself from breaking.

At playtime, while teachers smiled in other directions,

the girls used her as a target.

They shoved her.

Pushed her to the ground.

Trampled her back as she curled up, face buried in her arms.

Her hair collected dust.

Her knees gathered cuts.

But she said nothing.

After school, if they walked home together, the words came sharper:

"You don't even have a dad."

"No wonder you wear old clothes."

"Charity case."

Tien didn't respond.

She just walked — quietly, deliberately —

like her silence was the only shield she had.

Eventually, she found a way to avoid them.

She would stay back after class, pretending to tidy her desk,

waiting until the room emptied and the girls had gone ahead.

When Le asked why she was coming home late,

Tien smiled and said,

"The teacher likes me. Sometimes she keeps me back to talk."

Le beamed with pride.

And Tien didn't have the heart to tell her the truth.

At home, she kept the bruises to herself.

Not because she didn't trust Le —

but because she loved her too much.

Le had so little time.

And Tien had already taken enough space in her day.

But that didn't mean she didn't feel.

One afternoon, she stood near the sewing machine while Le chatted with a customer.

The woman said,

"Your girl — so polite, so quiet.

Mine says she never cries, even when other kids are mean."

Tien looked at her shoes.

Le didn't seem surprised.

She just smiled faintly.

"She doesn't cry," she said.

"But that doesn't mean she doesn't feel."

And in that moment, something shifted inside Tien.

Not a hardening. Not a fire.

Just a small, steady warmth.

The kind that says: I'm still here.

The kind that stays — even when words don't.

She didn't grow hatred, nor wish them harm.

She carried something stronger than anger:

She carried her silence like steel.

That evening, the house was dim, warm with the scent of rice and soy.

Tien came home a little later than usual — slower steps, heavier shoulders.

Le didn't ask questions.

She simply placed a bowl on the table:

Steamed rice.

A fried egg with crispy edges.

A few sprigs of boiled greens.

Tien sat down.

For a moment, they didn't speak.

Then Le gently pushed the egg closer to her daughter's side.

"You need this more than me," she said softly.

Tien looked up.

Le didn't know the details — but she knew enough.

And something loosened inside her.

Not the pain. Not yet.

But the belief that she didn't have to hold it all alone.

She picked up her spoon.

Scooped a bit of rice.

Took a slow bite.

The egg was warm.

The rice soft.

The greens a little bitter.

But together,

they tasted like being seen.

Chapter 6
Peace
And the Quiet That Grew Things

Le had grown tired —

not of sewing, but of waiting.

She realised that no matter how many hours she worked,

it would take years to leave the neighbourhood.

So she did something brave.

With a portion of her savings,

she began lending small sums to women who sold vegetables,

fish, and fabric scraps at the market.

Her heart trembled at first.

But she chose to believe in their honesty.

It worked.

The money came back with interest.

And for the first time in years, the meals got bigger.

Not extravagant — just enough.

A bit more rice, sometimes an egg, sometimes a second fish.

The nights grew quieter too.

Le still worked,

but now she allowed herself to stop when her eyes grew heavy.

Sometimes, just before bed,

she told Tien stories from a life that smelled of straw and smoke.

"When I was your age," she whispered once,

"I watched cows in the rice fields.

We didn't bring lunch — too poor.

But we'd find cassava in neighbours' gardens — everyone had it.

We'd ask, and they gave. We'd dig with our hands

and burn it with dried rice straw.

The skin turned black like coal."

Tien's eyes widened.

"But inside," Le continued,

"when you peel it off — white, sweet, warm.

Like eating smoke and sunlight."

Tien giggled.

"That's poor-people cake."

Le laughed.

"The best kind."

That night, with full bellies and stories in the air,

the house no longer felt so small.

The next morning was a day off for Tien.

She helped Le with the sewing — a peaceful day to her.

Le stood folding clothes with a neighbour,

sipping weak tea from chipped cups.

Tien sat nearby, sorting thread by colour.

A woman arrived to collect her áo dài —

a deep plum silk with a hand-stitched collar.

Her eyes were kind, but her voice carried news.

"Did you hear about the wedding in Ba Hamlet?" she asked.

Le raised an eyebrow.

"Cancelled?"

The woman nodded.

"Cold feet?"

"No. Fortune teller.

Same one my cousin went to — she's famous.

Said if they marry, one will die young."

Le's hand paused over the cloth.

She didn't speak. Just nodded faintly.

Tien listened quietly, fingers looping thread,

not yet understanding — but storing it away.

The customer shook her head.

"Imagine — months of planning, money already spent, and now it's off.

They say fate can't be tricked."

The conversation drifted on,

but the words stayed with Tien longer than the tea.

She didn't yet know

how those whispers would one day touch her own life.

Chapter 7
Mila
And the Loyalty That Couldn't Be Saved

৯৯

When Tien was eight, a cousin gifted her a dog named Mila.

At school — where others mocked her patched clothes and quiet nature —

Mila became her defender.

He walked beside her like a shadow, barking when strangers came too close.

One summer, she pretended to drown in the lake as a prank.

Mila, not knowing, leapt in and swam to her.

Laughter followed.

Love echoed through the trees.

Though the neighbourhood hadn't improved —

Le had just been cheated in a bad loan —

Tien carried on with quiet devotion.

School, chores, then time with Mila.

Le worked late.

But Mila stayed.

Until one day, he didn't.

After school, Mila didn't greet her at the front door.

Tien rushed inside.

"Mum?"

Le stood facing the wall.

"Where's Mila?"

Her voice barely rose.

"Don't go outside."

"Why?"

A pause.

"They're… they're cooking Mila. At the neighbour's house."

"I tried to stop them."

Tien froze.

No scream.

No tears.

Just silence.

She dropped her backpack and stormed next door.

Hot pot steaming.

Rice wine poured.

The neighbour's mid-meal.

No one met her eyes.

She stood there — still, staring —

then turned back when Le gently called her home.

"Tell me everything," Tien said.

Le didn't turn around. She kept cutting fabric. Her voice trembled.

"I hadn't seen Mila for a while.

I heard a scream, but… I didn't think it was him.

Then I saw the neighbour's friends near the river, hiding a bag.

Later, his fur — on their kitchen floor."

Tien's body trembled.

Anger.

Helplessness.

A grief too big to name.

That night, they didn't eat.

Only the hum of the sewing machine filled the room — punctuated by mourning.

Later, Le placed a bowl of minced pork congee on the table.

"I made extra. I know you used to save your portion for him."

She didn't wait for a reply.

Just walked back to her machine.

42

Tien sat. The congee steamed softly.

She picked it up and held it to her chest.

A tear slid down — but she didn't brush it away.

Before dawn, with the sky still bruised from sleep,

Tien stirred at the sound of oil crackling.

She tiptoed into the kitchen.

Le stood at the stove, flipping a shallot omelette. Her eyes were red.

"Mum," Tien whispered.

Le turned, blinking.

"What happened to your eyes?"

"Oh… it's the onion," she said, wiping her cheek.

"There's no onion in the omelette."

A pause.

"Must've been a long sewing night."

Tien nodded.

"Can you show me where they hid Mila? The tide is up."

They walked together through the grey morning.

Past the rusted fence.

The river moved slowly, as if it mourned too.

Le pointed near the reeds.

Tien pulled a small paper boat from her pocket —

the one she'd folded before dawn.

"Rest now, Mila," she whispered.

"There's no more pain. I'll see you later."

She knelt by the water and placed the boat on the surface.

It floated gently in the first light —

dancing with the current,

carrying her love downstream.

Chapter 8
Home, When He's Here
And the Shoulders That Carried Her Higher

Life always felt lighter when Minh came home from university.

His footsteps in the house, his voice at the dinner table,

the way he teased Le while washing rice —

everything felt a little easier.

A little safer.

He knew about the bullying, even if Tien hadn't said much.

He noticed how she flinched when certain names came up.

How she avoided walking home with others.

"Don't tell Mum," he said once, crouching beside her as she packed her schoolbag.

"She's already got so much on her plate. You're strong. I know you are."

And somehow, hearing that from him made it easier to keep going.

Tien's happiest moments were beside him — especially when they flew kites.

Hers were always homemade: newspaper, bamboo sticks, string that frayed too easily.

They never flew high. Sometimes they barely lifted off the ground.

But she didn't care.

What mattered was the wind in her hair,

the feel of the earth beneath her feet,

the scent of thick grass.

She'd run until her lungs burned,

laughing as her kite spun and tangled behind her.

Minh never scolded her.

He stood on the dike, arms crossed, grinning wide.

"Run faster," he'd shout.

"You'll lift it!"

When he was home, no one mocked her.

The whispers stopped.

The pushing faded.

The isolation dissolved in his presence.

To Tien, Minh wasn't just a sibling.

He was a shield.

Proof to the world that she wasn't alone.

And in those kite-flying days,

when the string tugged gently at her wrist

and the sky hovered just out of reach,

she didn't mind.

The air was full of freedom.

And her heart, full of peace.

That year, the family got a black-and-white television —

an old one that flickered and buzzed, powered by a charger wired carefully to the wall.

But it worked.

And that was enough.

They'd sit on the floor — Minh, Tien, and Le — shoulders brushing in the dim light.

Le would bring out a bowl of roasted peanuts, tossed with salt and crushed lime leaves.

The scent filled the air — nutty, citrusy, a little smoky.

The crunch of each bite matched the hum of the old TV.

Sometimes, a neighbour might pause by the open door, drawn by the glow and sound.

A few would slip in, find a spot on the floor, and stay.

No need to knock.

This was a house people felt welcome in.

There were no recliners.

No sofa.

Just mats, plastic fans creaking in the heat,

and the soft click of peanuts falling into the empty tin bowl.

But the nights were cosy.

And to Tien, they felt like a celebration —

of being together,

of having enough,

of knowing that for once,

there was nothing to run from.

One evening, after dinner, Tien sat beside Minh under the fading porch light.

The village was quiet — just broom strokes and a few barking dogs in the distance.

She looked down, fiddling with the string on her shorts.

"I'm saving up," she said without a sound.

"I want to move out of this neighbourhood one day.

Maybe to the town where the good school is."

Minh looked at her, surprised.

She rarely spoke of dreams.

"I'm going to be top of my class," she added.

"If I study hard, maybe they'll stop bullying me."

Minh was quiet for a moment, then nodded.

"That's a good plan," he said gently.

"You're smart enough. And strong enough."

He bumped her shoulder lightly.

"And if anyone gives you trouble — just remember,

they're not the ones flying kites with you."

One morning, as the village stirred with broom strokes and cooking smoke,

Minh sat beside her on the front step.

"Is there anyone who bullies you that lives nearby?" he asked, pulling on his flip-flops.

Tien's eyes widened.

"Yes… one of them lives just a few houses away."

Minh stood, dusted his pants, and crouched with a grin.

"Alright then. Get on.

I'll carry you on my shoulders. Let them see you have a strong guardian."

Tien blinked, then climbed on.

Her arms wrapped around his forehead.

Her body rose high above the dusty road.

As they walked the neighbourhood, people looked up.

Some smiled. Some raised eyebrows.

But Minh just kept walking — proud and steady.

Tien felt taller than the houses.

Not because she wanted revenge.

Not to frighten anyone.

But because — for the first time — she felt claimed.

Protected.

Lifted.

Loved.

It wasn't about scaring bullies.

It was about saying, to someone – "I'm not alone"

That night, rain tapped the leaf roof — a steady rhythm like a lullaby.

The old TV flickered in the corner.

Le set down a bowl of roasted peanuts, warm and salted,

the scent of lime leaf rising into the room.

Minh sat beside Tien on the mat, shoulders touching.

The room was dim, but full —

of comfort, laughter, and the quiet joy that only comes

when the world outside is wet and cold,

but inside, you are known and safe.

Outside, a forgotten kite hung from a tree branch — soaked, limp.

But Tien didn't mind.

The sky may not have lifted it that day.

But something in her heart had already flown.

Chapter 9
The Bitterness in Sweet & Sour
And the Quiet Gift That Cost Everything

৶

Tien was nine when her world shifted —

not with noise, but with silence.

Things happened the day Le's biggest customer finally confessed

she couldn't repay the money.

Years of trust.

Hours of sewing.

Most of their savings — gone in a single afternoon.

Le collapsed quietly in the sewing corner,

her hands slack, her back hunched over a pile of unfinished fabric.

The sewing machine was still on, humming faintly.

But Le's hands didn't move.

One thread dangled from the needle —

loose and unfinished, like a sentence left unsaid.

Tien stood in the doorway, frozen.

She had never seen Le like that —

so still, so emptied.

No scolding. No sighing.

Just silence that felt like it could swallow the whole house.

She walked with hush to her room,

pulled open the bottom drawer of the old cabinet,

and reached for her ceramic pig.

It was heavy —

not with wealth, but with effort.

Coins she had saved from lunch money,

tucked away with the small hope

that maybe, someday, she could help them leave the mafia neighbourhood.

It was a childish dream,

but one she believed in with all her heart.

The ceramic pig didn't just hold coins.

It held her hopes.

Every clink inside was a quiet dream that one day, they'd leave this place.

She didn't hesitate.

Dreams could be rebuilt.

But Le needed strength now.

She held the pig in both hands,

stared at it a long moment,

then gently smashed it against the tile floor.

The ceramic cracked in two.

Coins scattered like raindrops.

She gathered them, counted them carefully,

and brought them to Le.

"Mum," she whispered,

"this is my saving. See if it helps a bit… with the money they stole from you."

Le turned to her daughter,

eyes red, hands trembling.

She looked at the pile of small coins and then back at Tien.

"No, that doesn't count, honey," she said, trying to steady her voice.

"I appreciate it. But keep it for yourself."

Tien paused, then nodded solemnly.

"Then you'll have to buy me a new ceramic pig. I broke mine."

Le's mouth quivered at the edges.

No tears. Just that quiet ache only a mother knows.

Later that day, Minh came home from town.

It wasn't planned.

Maybe he felt something in his bones.

Or maybe the timing was a kindness from the world.

His presence was like a door opening —

letting in fresh air,

and just enough strength for Le to stand again.

The house was still heavy with silence,

but Tien, trying to lift it, said with a smile,

"Let's make sweet & sour soup… for Brother."

Everyone knew it was her favourite.

She asked it that way because kindness often finds its way through a small lie.

Minh frowned, his voice low.

"Tien, don't ask for things. We don't have much money now."

But Le stood up slowly, brushing the threads off her lap.

"We have enough," she said softly.

"I'll go buy the ingredients."

The scent of pineapple and tamarind filled the kitchen,

rising with steam and memory.

Tien watched every step —

how Le handled the fish with care,

how the herbs were tossed in like blessings.

The sound of the soup bubbling was the closest thing to comfort.

At the dinner table, there was only one piece of fish —

set gently in Tien's bowl.

She looked around. Minh only had broth and vegetables.

Le, too.

The soup was perfect. Sweet, sour, warm. Just the way she loved it.

But as she chewed the fish her mother placed in her bowl,

something new bloomed behind the flavour: guilt.

Le had poured her strength into this bowl.

Not for herself.

For Tien.

And that's when she understood:

Love sacrifices quietly,

even when no one's watching.

After dinner, while Minh washed the dishes, Tien walked quietly to the sewing table, where Le was stitching in silence.

"Mum," she said softly,

"I'm sorry for asking for the soup. I promise I won't ask for anything from now on. We don't have much money."

Le looked up from the fabric, her eyes glassy with unshed tears.

She didn't speak at first —

just watched her daughter standing there,

guilt far too big for her age.

In that moment, she saw it clearly:

The world had pressed too much into this little girl's heart.

That a bowl of sweet and sour fish soup could feel like a luxury —

that broke something inside Le more than the debt ever could.

She reached out, touched Tien's cheek, and said only,

"You never need to be sorry for being loved."

Chapter 10
Muffins and Misunderstandings
And the Gift That Said More Than Words

ᥫᦫ

After being cheated out of most of her savings,

Le knew there wasn't time to grieve.

Grief would have to wait.

Her hands returned to the fabric.

Her mind, to measurements and stitches.

And so she rose — slowly, steadily,

with quiet determination — like a phoenix among ashes.

Customers still came.

Her skill spoke louder than circumstance.

Tien, now a little older, became her mother's helper and shadow.

She was the deliverer — bringing cut pieces to the overlocker shop and back again.

Villagers knew her —

the little girl with a bag bigger than herself,

lifting it above the dirt path so it wouldn't drag.

On stormy days, her hair clung to her forehead.

On dry ones, dust covered her legs and face.

Some smiled.

Others admired her silently.

Even classmates — those who once mocked her — grew quiet

after their parents spoke of

"the girl who works harder than grown-ups."

Some days the load was too much.

She'd drag the bag, threads slipping from the tears.

She'd run back, heart pounding, to retrieve every piece.

No scrap was too small —

not when her mother called them "very important."

Le later taught her embroidery.

Tien stitched her own handkerchief while others brought store-bought ones.

Some classmates asked her to make one for them — for pay.

Tien told Le proudly, expecting praise.

But Le only shook her head.

"You can embroider for yourself.

But your time belongs to your studies now.

If you want to be the top, you must focus."

Then came Mother's Day.

Tien had just enough saving money for a bouquet… or a box of muffins.

She'd never dared buy muffins.

Not when that money could help her dream grow.

But this time, she thought,

Mum has never tried them. She should.

She handed over her coins, hands trembling with excitement.

The warm box in her arms felt like treasure.

The sun peeked through clouds.

The road home felt smoother.

She imagined it all:

Her mum's tired face lighting up.

The box opened slowly.

Maybe a story over tea.

Maybe a smile.

"Happy Mother's Day, Mum."

Tien held out the muffins with both hands, like a crown.

Le looked at the box.

Her face changed.

"Where did you get the money?" she asked, voice thin.

"Did you… steal it from me?"

She dropped her scissors and sank into the chair.

Tien froze.

"No, Mum. I saved my snack money.

I… I can return it if you don't like it."

Silence.

Just the fan creaking.

Cicadas buzzing.

The scent of earth through the window.

Le slowly lowered her hands.

Her gaze far away — not on the muffins,

but on years of weariness.

Tien stood frozen, box still in her hands,

no longer glowing with pride.

"I thought you'd be happy," she whispered.

Le looked at her then — really looked.

"Oh honey…" She reached out and pulled Tien close.

"I didn't mean to scare you. I was just… afraid.

Sometimes I worry so much, I forget what's in front of me.

I see you. I see all you're doing.

Thank you."

They sat like that a long time.

Later that evening, the muffins sat on a plate.

One missing.

Le had finally taken a bite.

She didn't say much. Just poured more tea.

But the silence felt softer than before.

Then the landline rang.

"Hello?"

It was Minh.

"Happy Mother's Day," he said when Le came to the phone.

Her voice cracked a little, but she quickly asked about his studies.

Tien waited, bouncing on her feet.

When Le passed her the receiver, Tien beamed.

"Minh! I bought muffins for Mum. She already ate one!

There's some left! Come home soon!"

Minh laughed.

"You did that? Good girl. I'll try to come this weekend."

"Promise?"

"I'll try."

Tien hung up with a smile, heart full.

The day hadn't gone as she imagined.

But the muffins were shared.

The silence softened.

And that, she thought, *was enough.*

Chapter 11
The Stitch That Holds
And the Thread That Doesn't Break

&

Tien was ten when the pain began.

At first, Le said it was her back — just a small ache.

But one evening, while sewing a collar, she collapsed.

She vomited. She couldn't move.

She lay in bed for days, sweat soaking the pillow, her body curled in pain.

Tien ran to the neighbour, then to the pharmacy,

clutching coins in one hand and a note with scribbled instructions in the other.

When the doctor came, he examined Le carefully and sighed.

"Kidney stones," he said.

"It will return. It always does."

The house fell quiet.

Tien became the host —

too small for her apron, but too brave to let things fall.

She swept the floor. Stirred rice over the fire.

Fetched water. Explained to her mother's customers why their clothes would be delayed.

When she was tired, when she was scared, she prayed.

Not loud. Not long. Just one sentence:

"God, please let Mum be okay."

One day, a woman came to the house — Mrs Thuy.

Her áo dài — perfectly made by Le before the illness — hung from her arm.

"This part is too tight," she said, pointing.

"And this seam… could have been better. I want a discount."

Tien's hands clenched. She stepped forward.

"My mum made the best áo dài in this area," she said sharply.

"You just want a discount!"

The room fell still.

Le, pale and weak, sat up slowly and motioned for her daughter.

In the hallway, her voice was soft, but her eyes were firm.

"Tien… where are your manners? She is our customer.

Remember what I taught you? They give us money — for food, for your school.

They expect the best. They deserve the best."

Tien's eyes filled.

Le placed a hand on her arm.

"I love my work. And I respect it.

That means I respect them, too.

Now go. Do what you need to do with her."

Tien walked back to the living room, heart heavy.

Mrs Thuy stood with her arms crossed, lips pursed.

Tien bowed her head.

"I'm sorry, Mrs Thuy.

I promise I'll never speak to you — or anyone — that way again.

You deserve the best áo dài from us."

Mrs Thuy blinked. Her face softened just a little.

She turned to Le.

"I won't ask for a discount. But please fix the bottom hem.

I want it a bit wider."

"I'll do it today," Le replied gently.

"Please come back tomorrow."

That night, while washing rice for dinner,

Tien looked over at her mother — still pale, still sewing.

And she realised: strength wasn't always loud.

Sometimes it was quiet.

Sometimes it bowed its head.

But it never stopped giving its best.

Le's pain didn't vanish overnight.

The medicine helped.

So did the warm compresses Tien made from old scarves and boiled water.

Each day, Le moved a little more.

Stitched a little longer.

Smiled a little deeper.

That afternoon, the jasmine-like scent of kumquat blossoms drifted through the window.

Tien set up two plastic chairs and a small table under the tree,

as they always did when they needed a breath of peace.

She poured jasmine tea into chipped porcelain cups.

Le came slowly out to sit beside her — shoulders tired, but eyes grateful.

"Smells like New Year," Le whispered, closing her eyes.

"Smells like you're still strong," Tien smiled.

Each night, as the sky turned blue-grey, Tien sat at her keyboard.

Soft melodies filled the house —

not perfect, not complex.

Just enough to wrap around the walls like comfort.

Le listened from the sewing room.

Sometimes she hummed.

Sometimes she closed her eyes and let the music carry her

somewhere far from pain.

That night, as the music faded into silence, Tien slipped into the kitchen.

She lit a small flame and placed a pot on the stove.

From the basket, she pulled a small piece of fresh fish.

She peeled ginger with careful fingers,

sliced spring onion, and washed the rice twice until the water ran clear.

Soon, the scent of fish congee filled the house —

gentle, soothing, with steam curling up like prayer.

When it was done, she brought a bowl to her mother's bedside.

Le smiled, too tired to speak, and took a slow spoonful.

Tien sat beside her, resting her head against the wall.

She didn't say it aloud. She didn't need to.

"God, let this help her heal."

The night went on quietly.

And for the first time in days,

Le slept peacefully.

Chapter 12
The Braised Fish
And the Bite That Wasn't Thrown Away

ॐ

There was only a small piece left.

The braised fish sat in the centre of the table,

glistening in its dark, fragrant sauce.

Dinner was finished.

Tien wiped her mouth with a napkin, looked at the last bite, and said softly,

"Just throw it away, Mum. It's not enough to keep."

Le paused.

Then, gently:

"You know, your brother once swam across a river

with only a piece of water coconut tied to his chest…

just to bring home fish."

Tien looked up.

Le smiled faintly, the memory already in her eyes.

"It was flood season," she said.

"I told him not to go. The river was big. The current was fast.

But he found a piece of net — someone had thrown it away — and tied it around his belly.

Then he hugged that water coconut trunk and swam across, all the way to the other side."

She paused

"He was just eight or nine," Le added quietly.

"Too small for the river — but he went anyway."

She shook her head lightly, as if seeing it again.

"He came back soaked through. His teeth were chattering, and his lips were blue.

But he was grinning. He laid two little fish on the table,

with a bunch of wild spinach, and said, 'We'll eat tonight.'"

Tien stayed quiet.

Le's voice softened.

"I made braised fish that night. Just fish sauce, sugar, and salt.

We didn't even have rice. I boiled the greens, and we sat down to eat.

No one said anything. We just dipped vegetables in the sauce."

She gave a small laugh.

"I said, 'I don't like fish.'

And he said, 'Neither do I.'

But when we finished, the sauce was gone — and those two little fish were still sitting in the pot."

Le looked at Tien now, gently.

"The next morning, I added more water. A bit more fish sauce.

He brought back more greens, and we ate again.

We did that for almost a week.

Those two fish kept us full — just enough."

Her voice cracked slightly, like the memory itself had aged with her.

Tien sat very still.

The plate of braised fish hadn't moved,

but it felt different now.

It wasn't just food anymore.

It was a story.

A life.

A reminder that the things we waste once cost someone everything.

She picked up the last piece,

wrapped it gently,

and placed it in the food cupboard.

"I'll eat it tomorrow," she said.

Le nodded once.

Neither said more.

The fish was safe.

The memory was honoured.

And something had been passed from mother to daughter —

without a single lesson spoken aloud.

Chapter 13
The Sweet Fruit
And the Smile That Said, We Did It

❧

By Year Five, it had been three years since Tien told her brother and mother,

"I want to be the top of my class so no one will bully me anymore."

Now, she had done it.

She had studied through long nights, hunched under the yellow light of her desk lamp.

She had listened more than she spoke, memorised more than required, and carried her quiet ambition like a shield.

Slowly, the teasing faded.

Being first meant something.

It meant leadership.

It meant respect.

Even those who once mocked her spoke more gently — curious now, instead of cruel.

On the final day of school, Tien turned to Le.

"You should come today, Mum. There's… a surprise."

Le hesitated — there was always work.

But something in Tien's voice made her put down the scissors that morning.

She dressed modestly, combed her hair, and sat quietly in the audience, folding her hands in her lap.

Then she heard it:

Tien's name — called through the microphone.

First place in the year.

A pause. Applause.

A few murmurs of surprise.

Le's eyes welled — not with "onion tears," but something deeper.

Something earned.

From the stage, Tien turned – and met her mother's eyes – before walking forward.

She looked at her mother and smiled.

Not the shy smile of a child seeking approval —

but the proud smile that said, We did it.

Le smiled back.

In that moment, the world outside disappeared.

They walked home side by side beneath the early summer sun.

The dusty road felt lighter.

Birds sang a little louder.

The leaves stirred like applause.

Along the narrow lanes, whispers followed them —

not cruel ones this time.

"That's the girl from the tailor's house."

"The quiet one."

"The one with no father."

"She topped the year."

Tien heard them.

Le did too.

But neither looked back.

At home, Le asked,

"What would you like to eat?"

Tien grinned.

"Duck curry. With taro."

Le laughed.

"Your favourite. Let's make it together."

The house filled with warm, familiar smells —

the rich fragrance of duck simmering in curry paste,

the earthy sweetness of taro melting into the sauce,

the soft hiss of coconut milk bubbling.

Tien stood beside her mother, chopping herbs, stirring gently, smiling.

It wasn't a feast.

It wasn't shared with guests.

But it was theirs.

That night, with bowls of curry and rice between them,

they didn't need words.

Just glances.

Just pride.

Just a flavour that said: This moment is ours. And we earned it.

Later, with the curry still simmering on the stove, Le picked up the landline and dialled.

"Minh," she said, already bright with pride.

"She did it. Your sister — first in her class."

On the other end, Minh's voice lifted through the static:

"I knew she would. Put her on, Mum."

Le handed the phone to Tien, who hesitated — shy, glowing.

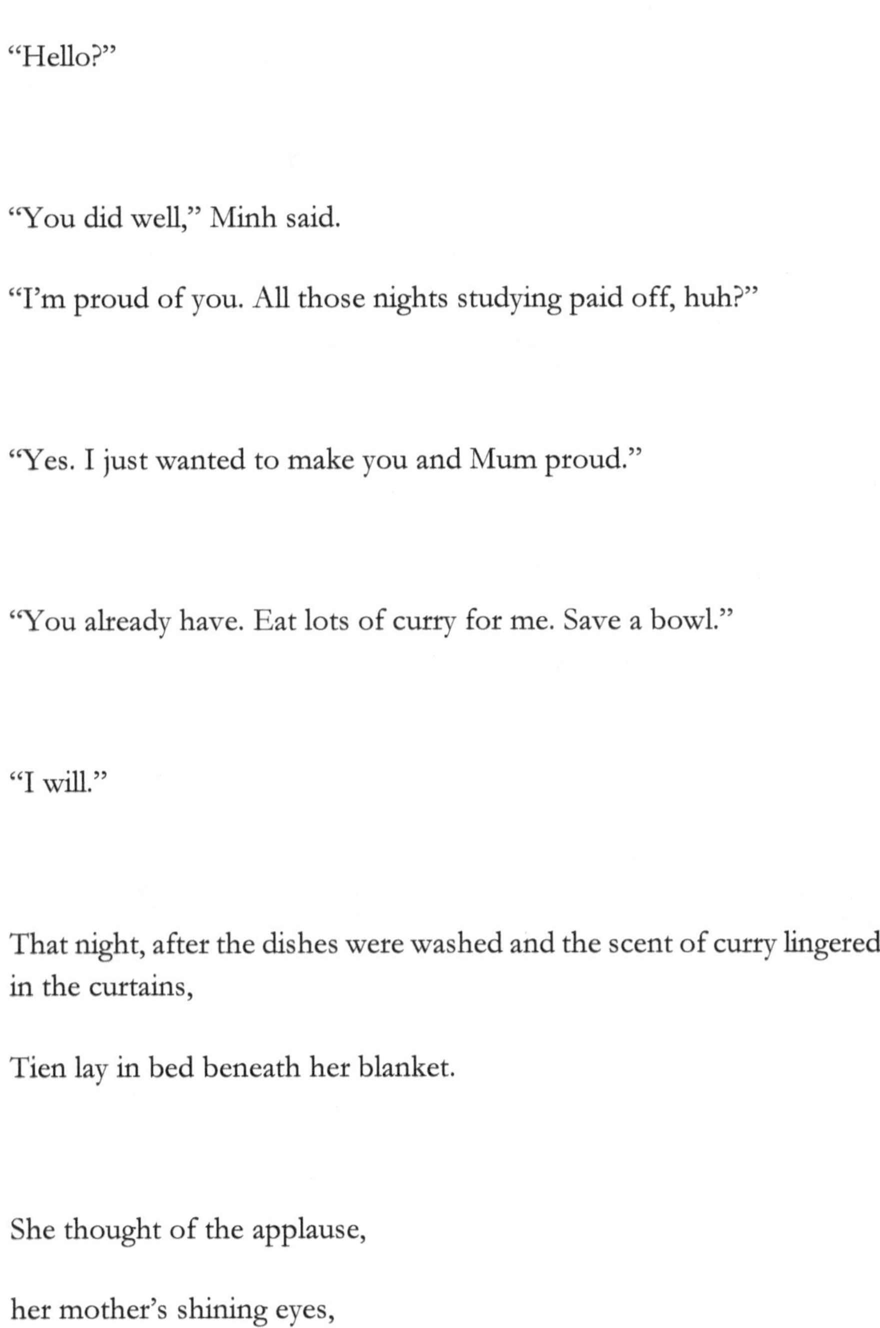

"Hello?"

"You did well," Minh said.

"I'm proud of you. All those nights studying paid off, huh?"

"Yes. I just wanted to make you and Mum proud."

"You already have. Eat lots of curry for me. Save a bowl."

"I will."

That night, after the dishes were washed and the scent of curry lingered in the curtains,

Tien lay in bed beneath her blanket.

She thought of the applause,

her mother's shining eyes,

her brother's voice — steady and proud.

For the first time in a long while, she didn't fall asleep worrying what others thought.

She closed her eyes, heart full, and whispered:

"Today, I didn't just survive. I stood tall."

And the world, for once, stood still to notice.

Chapter 14
The Librarian
And the Silence That Was Not Empty

&

Now in Year Six, Tien still held her place at the top of the class.

Each day, she returned from school, changed out of her uniform, and stepped into another role — her mother's little apprentice.

While Le sat at the sewing machine, Tien ironed the freshly stitched garments — careful with every crease, folding them just right, hanging them in neat rows for the customers.

She knew which pieces belonged to whom without reading the name tags.

Her eyes caught the shape. Her hands remembered the fabric.

She didn't speak much.

Not because she lacked words —

but because there was often no one to hear them.

Her mother was always working.

Her brother, away.

Mila, gone.

At school, she smiled when spoken to, answered politely, but rarely started conversations.

Children noticed.

Some mistook her quiet for strangeness.

Others simply left her alone.

So books became her companions.

Her father — during one of his rare, unannounced visits — brought what she asked for:

science books filled with planets, circuits, and unfamiliar machines.

Later, English books and CDs, so she could understand the voices on the radio and in the streets.

She wanted to learn. To move forward.

To belong in more than one world.

No one ever offered her fiction — no storybooks about princesses or talking animals.

When she did find one, she read it slowly, savouring every page like a rare fruit.

In books, no one mocked her.

No one hurt her.

No one asked her to explain herself.

She could be someone.

A reader. A learner. A dreamer.

She didn't need a crowd.

Only a page.

Every break, while other students laughed and whispered outside,

she slipped between the rows of bookshelves.

She wasn't looking for company.

She was looking for possibility.

Most students walked past the science section like it was dust.

But Tien was drawn to it — those shelves no one touched, except the teachers.

The old librarian noticed.

Her name was Mrs Linh.

She had worked at the school longer than anyone could remember.

Hair always in a low bun.

Glasses resting halfway down her nose.

Voice soft as turning pages.

At first, she only watched.

Then one day, she said gently,

"You like the ones no one reads."

Tien nodded.

After that, a quiet bond formed.

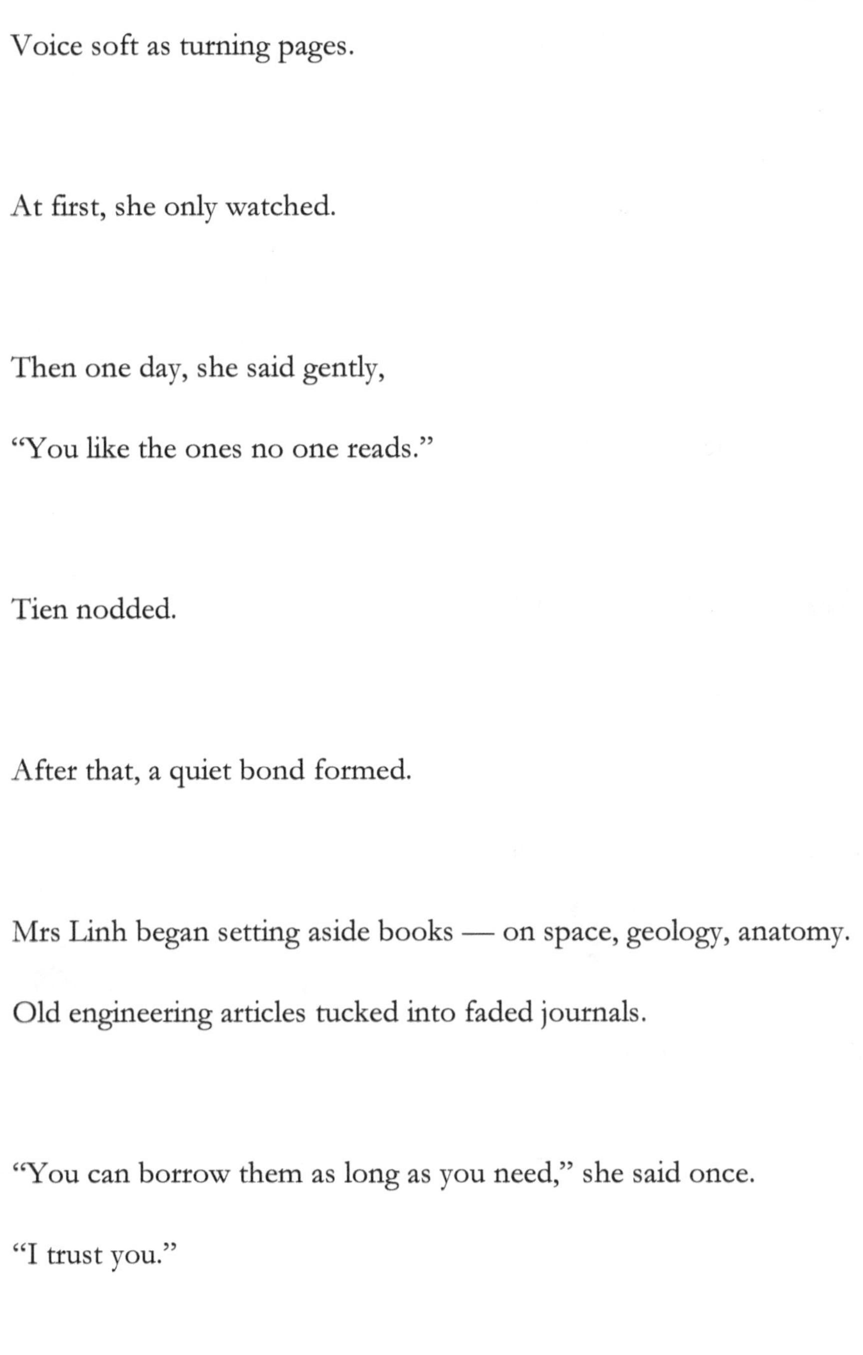

Mrs Linh began setting aside books — on space, geology, anatomy.

Old engineering articles tucked into faded journals.

"You can borrow them as long as you need," she said once.

"I trust you."

Tien always returned them — clean, marked only by memory.

Mrs Linh also knew about the bullying.

She never said it aloud,

but her kindness came in other ways.

She never asked why Tien didn't eat.

Never commented on why she came alone.

Sometimes, she would place a wrapped snack on the desk, just within reach.

"You can eat here," she'd say, pretending to look away.

Tien never forgot that.

In a world full of noise,

Mrs Linh made space for her silence.

And in the pages of forgotten books,

Tien found more than knowledge.

She found someone who noticed.

Chapter 15
The Quiet Flame
And the First Lesson at the Stove

ॐ

After school, the quiet didn't end at the library doors.

It followed Tien home — where books gave way to recipes,

and learning took on a new shape beneath her mother's watchful eye.

One warm afternoon, while Le was preparing lunch,

Tien looked up and asked,

"Mum, can you teach me how to cook, please?

I can cook while you work."

Le was slicing lemongrass into thin rings.

She paused, then turned with a soft smile.

"I can teach you. But be very careful with the chair and the electric cooker.

Always remember — the pan is hot."

Tien grabbed a small plastic stool and placed it near the stove.

She climbed up carefully — just tall enough to reach the pan.

That day, Le was making her comfort dish:

pan-fried pork chop with lemongrass.

The kitchen filled with the scent of home —

lemongrass sizzling in oil, sweet soy sauce caramelising at the pork's edges,

the gentle earthiness of crushed garlic.

The heat coaxed the fragrance into the air like a melody rising from silence.

Tien took a deep breath.

The smell alone made her feel full of love.

They only cooked once a day — to save time, to save power.

This meal would be for both lunch and dinner.

The table was set with simple perfection:

golden pork chops on a ceramic plate, fresh cucumber slices in a small dish,

and a bowl of soy sauce with chopped red chilli floating like petals on dark water.

Le brought over the rice pot, its lid hissing gently with steam.

As they ate, Le — as always — told a story.

"When I was at the old house," she said, picking up a piece of pork,

"there was a neighbour — kind-hearted.

Some night, when your grandma had gone to sleep,

she came quietly and gave me firewood."

Tien paused mid-bite.

"Why only at night?"

"Because if others saw her helping us, they would mock her.

But she never gave up. Poor lady…

she helped us every way she could."

Tien looked down at her rice, then up again, her eyes glowing — not just from pride, but from the quiet fire of wanting to become someone kind.

"When I grow up, I'll be a good-heart person like her."

Le reached out and tucked a strand of hair behind her daughter's ear.

"Yes, you will, darling. You already are."

Chapter 16
The Price of Light
And the Cost She Didn't Expect

છે

Year 7 came with pride —

and pressure.

Tien still held her place at the top:

leading the maths team, the physics group, the English support program, and even the drums.

Kind, calm, and steady — she helped others rise.

But leadership didn't protect her body.

One afternoon, while guiding an English group,

the words on the board began to blur.

The light pierced.

Her eyes wept without warning.

She blinked — once, twice —

but the tears wouldn't stop.

"Sorry," she whispered, slipping out of the room.

The walk home was painful.

The sun she once loved now burned.

The doctor was kind.

"Conjunctivitis," he said.

"It will heal."

But it didn't — not really.

The pain returned.

So did absence.

Her name was removed from the leadership boards —

first one group, then another.

"You're not reliable with time," a teacher said gently.

Tien nodded. Eyes lowered.

Not from shame — but from pain.

Her bag felt heavier.

Not with books,

but with silence.

At home, her mother was ironing.

Tien paused at the porch, unsure how to speak.

Before she could, the phone rang.

From inside, Le's voice floated out:

"Yes, thank you. We need the money for Tien's eyes.

She's seeing a specialist. Very expensive…"

Tien stood frozen.

Her eyes — the drops, the absences —

had cost more than she knew.

That night, she said nothing about school.

Just smiled.

"I'm home."

Le didn't know Tien had overheard the phone call. She simply nodded,

"Hi honey, go get changed, then come help with the soup."

Tien came to the kitchen; the scent of soup drifted through the house —

carrot, radish, pork ribs. Comfort in steam.

"Carrot is good for your eyes," Le said.

"Doctor told me."

Tien stood on the small plastic stool, stirring garlic.

She watched the vegetables swirl like boats in a quiet sea.

She tried to hum like her mum usually did.

Her voice cracked awkwardly.

From the sewing room, Le called out, laughing,

"Keep your practice down please — I can't sew when I'm giggling!"

Tien laughed too. But her gaze lingered on the sewing table.

The lamp stayed on longer these days. More fabric piled up.

Le was working harder — not for bills,

but for her daughter's eyes.

The next morning, Tien handed back her lunch money.

"I don't like school snacks anymore, Mum. I'll drink water."

Le didn't argue.

That evening, her cousin arrived —

holding a fluffy little dog.

He scratched his neck and said gently,

"Thought she could use some company."

He knew about the eyes.

The pain.

The absences.

From across the fence, Mrs Ba, their neighbour called:

"Tien! Don't name your dog Mila again!

Every time you call it, I think someone's yelling my name!"

Tien blinked.

"Why?"

"Mila, Mrs Ba — it sounds the same when you shout!

I keep answering for no reason!"

Everyone laughed.

Even Le chuckled behind the sewing machine.

"That's half a joke, half a real complaint."

And so, Mila became Milu.

He stayed.

So did the soup.

So did the sewing.

So did the light.

Even if Tien couldn't always see it.

Chapter 17
The Confession
And the Kindness That Came After

୬

Morning light crept through the small window,

spilling across the kitchen tiles.

It was the second day,

and still, Le didn't know the truth.

Tien's heart felt heavy —

each step weighted like stone.

She entered the kitchen and found a quiet surprise:

a warm pack of sticky rice

and a cool bottle of water waiting on the table.

Le looked up with a smile.

"Eat up before it gets cold."

Tien sat down, voice soft.

"Mum… next time, let me do that.

I'll buy breakfast for you. I'll prepare your water and tea."

Le grinned, lifting her cup.

"Then you'll have to wake up a bit earlier, darling."

She winked.

Tien managed a laugh.

The weight was still there — but lighter, for a moment.

At school, she walked with her head down,

careful not to meet anyone's eyes.

She feared the look she remembered from years ago —

the one that said: you're nothing now.

She reached her desk quietly and sat.

Then, a hand touched her shoulder.

She turned.

It was a classmate from her old maths team.

"Hey, Tien… my seat's closer to the board.

It's easier to see. Want to swap?"

Before she could answer, another voice chimed in:

"No — swap with me. Mine doesn't face the sun.

Better for your eyes."

Then another:

"Tien, I'll write down everything the teacher puts on the board for you."

"No, my handwriting is neater," someone added.

She laughed a little, overwhelmed.

"Tien, you don't have to clean the floor anymore — we'll take turns."

"And no more cleaning the board. Dust isn't good for your eyes."

The voices came like a chorus —

not rushed, not rehearsed — just real.

Care poured over her like sunlight through leaves.

She smiled, and tears welled —

this time, not from pain.

Someone noticed.

"Stop, stop! You're making her cry!"

"No good, no good!"

"Tien, don't worry. We're with you."

It was the first time she had felt this kind of love.

Not earned by marks.

Not won by leading groups.

Not paid for with silence.

Just love.

Freely given.

And in that moment, she realised something new:

She mattered —

not for what she did,

but for who she was.

She had braced for loneliness.

But the world had softened instead.

That evening, the house was quiet again.

The hum of the sewing machine filled the living room like a lullaby,

the needle clicking softly into fabric.

Tien sat at the table, gently peeling a mandarin —

segment by segment, like steady breaths.

She glanced at her mother.

Le was squinting slightly. The lamp flickered overhead.

The lines around her eyes looked deeper.

Her hands moved with care, but also with tiredness.

Tien's chest ached.

Now, she told herself. *Now.*

She walked over and sat beside her,

placing the small plate of mandarin slices down.

"Mum…" she said softly.

Le looked up, smile easy.

"Yes, darling?"

Tien's voice trembled like a string being plucked.

"I'm… I'm not the group leader anymore."

Le paused. Her hands rested still.

Tien continued quickly, eyes already blurring.

"My marks went down.

My eyes hurt too much to see the board.

I missed classes… and they said I couldn't lead anymore.

I — I didn't want to tell you because… I know you're proud of me."

There was silence for a moment.

Not heavy. Just quiet.

Le reached out and gently held her hand — warm and steady.

"Tien," she said,

"I'm proud of you because you are mine.

Not because of the marks. Not because of the groups.

Just… because of you."

Tien dropped her head against her mother's arm,

letting herself cry.

"I'm sorry I didn't tell you earlier."

Le smiled softly, brushing the hair from her daughter's face.

"You told me now. That's what matters."

The sewing machine sat still for a while.

The lamp stopped flickering.

And for once, the light didn't hurt her eyes.

It warmed her heart instead.

Chapter 18
The Salted Fish
And the Choice She Never Spoke Aloud

૭

Minh came home from university with a quiet look on his face.

He didn't ask right away.

He waited until after dinner —

until the dishes were cleared and the sewing machine had fallen silent.

"Mum," he said, standing by the doorway,

"I need to pay the school fee next week."

Le paused mid-stitch.

She already knew.

Money had been tight for months.

Tien's eyes needed constant check-ups, special drops, new prescriptions.

Every dollar felt like a choice between one child's vision and another's future.

Still, she smiled softly.

"I'll have it for you before you go back next week."

Minh nodded. He didn't push.

Then, barely above a whisper:

"Cousin said… my dad's wealthy."

The air shifted.

Le looked up. Her hands trembled slightly in her lap.

That man — the one who once made promises,

who walked away for wealth and ease — lived just across town.

Close enough to send a letter. To ask a question. To care.

He never did.

She stood up, wiped her cheeks with the back of her hand,

and faced her son.

"Minh," she said gently but firmly,

"look at me."

He did.

"If your father ever truly wanted to care for you,

he would've done it long ago.

He's nearby. He knows where we live.

But he chose not to.

And that's not your fault."

Minh lowered his eyes.

He understood.

The silence between them was heavy — but not cold.

It held both grief and love.

Later that night, after Minh had gone to bed,

Le stood in the kitchen folding away the tablecloth.

The lamp flickered softly overhead.

She thought of the words once spoken at the gate —

Twice abandoned.

But they hadn't seen what she carried.

They hadn't known the full truth.

She had never been the one who walked away.

Sunday morning came.

Le placed a folded envelope in Minh's hand.

"Here. Your school fee.

And some extra for food."

Minh flipped through the notes and frowned.

"Mum… this is too much. I just need half."

Le raised an eyebrow.

"How can you survive on half?

You need proper food for your studying."

Minh grinned faintly.

"Can you give me some of your salted fish?

It lasts the whole week."

She laughed, wiping her eyes again.

In the kitchen, she packed a small container of her home-cured salted fish —

sharp, fragrant, full of flavour.

The kind only a mother gets right.

"Take the fish. And the money.

Don't argue."

Minh hugged her quietly and said nothing more.

Le stood in the doorway long after he left,

staring down the road, holding her breath against the ache.

Not because of what she gave.

But because of what they both still carried.

Chapter 19
The Shield
And the Quiet Love That Stood Up

&

That night, Tien stayed awake longer than usual.

She thought about what had happened.

Her mother hadn't scolded her.

Her friends hadn't turned away.

Instead, she was met with understanding.

And that… changed everything.

She lay on her back, eyes gently closed —

not from exhaustion, but from gratitude.

"I'm lucky." she whispered into the dark.

"So lucky."

But another thought followed:

I still need a way to study… a way that doesn't hurt my eyes.

That's when the idea came.

If she couldn't follow every lesson during the day,

she'd learn everything the night before.

That way, when her eyes began to sting in class,

she could rest — and still understand, still belong.

So she began a quiet routine.

Each evening, she opened her books,

took slow, careful notes,

and read ahead.

In class, she stopped copying from the board and simply listened.

When questions came, she answered clearly.

Her marks rose again.

Her results spoke for her.

Top of the class — again.

But no leadership titles.

Tien smiled to herself.

"That's okay. For now… this is enough."

The doctor gave one more instruction:

She must wear sunglasses in class and outdoors to protect her eyes.

It helped.

But it made her look different.

Too different.

Some classmates began to whisper.

They called her mud skipper.

They squinted, pressed their lips together,

and pretended they'd caught one in their nets when she passed.

They laughed.

She didn't.

Tien didn't complain.

She stayed back after class, tidied slowly,

and left only when most had gone.

She walked home later each day.

And Le noticed.

One evening, Le looked up from her sewing and saw the time.

Her needle paused.

She set her glasses down and placed the thread aside.

That day, Le walked to the school —

not during pick-up time,

not with anger,

but with calm, steady steps.

She asked to speak with the homeroom teacher.

She told the truth — clearly and respectfully.

"My daughter is sick," she said.

"She's trying very hard.

But your students are mocking her.

This isn't right."

The next morning, the teacher stepped into class.

Her voice was calm — but unshakably firm.

"From today forward, any comment — any gesture —

that mocks someone's illness or appearance will not be tolerated."

She didn't raise her voice.

She didn't name names.

But everyone heard.

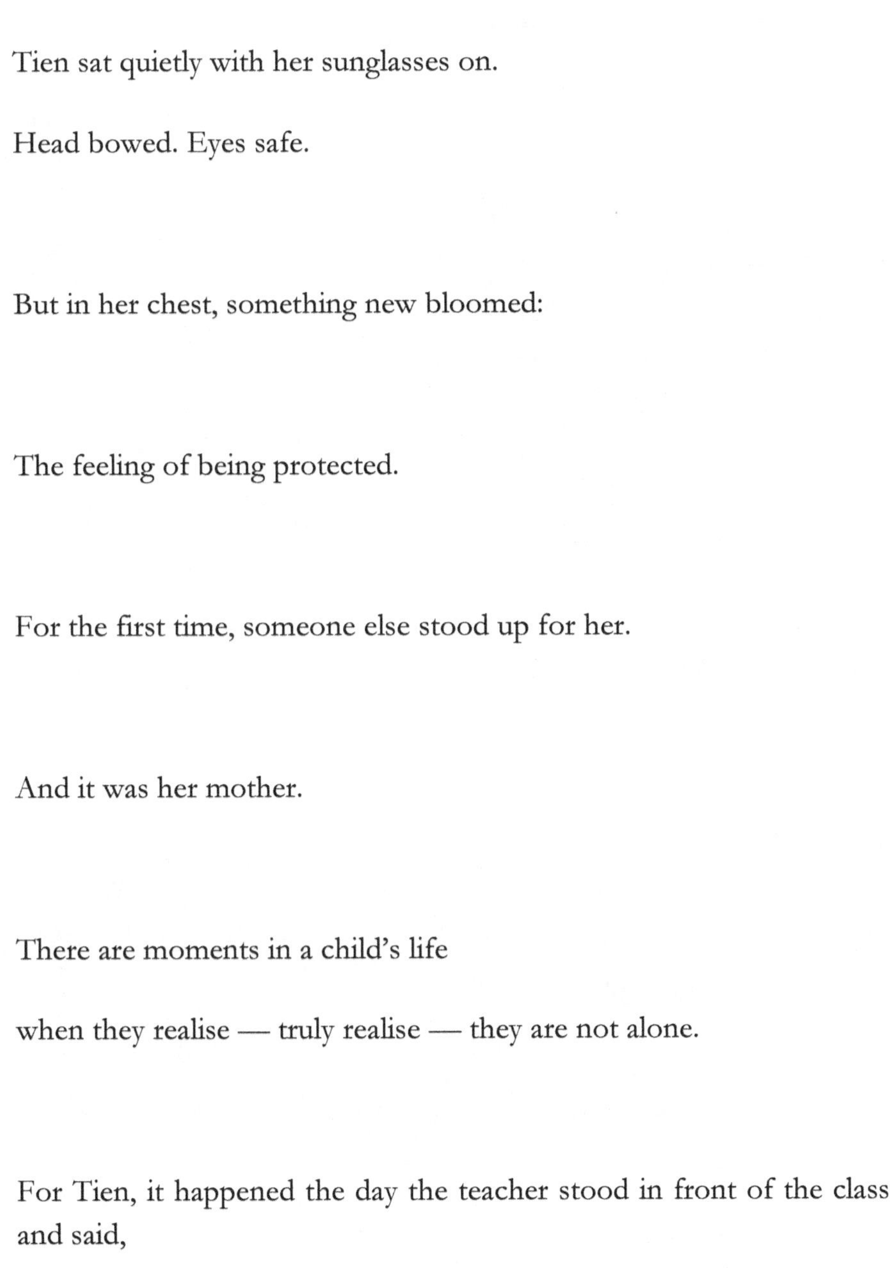

Tien sat quietly with her sunglasses on.

Head bowed. Eyes safe.

But in her chest, something new bloomed:

The feeling of being protected.

For the first time, someone else stood up for her.

And it was her mother.

There are moments in a child's life

when they realise — truly realise — they are not alone.

For Tien, it happened the day the teacher stood in front of the class and said,

"Any comment — any gesture — that mocks someone's illness or appearance will not be tolerated."

It wasn't loud.

It wasn't dramatic.

But it echoed like thunder inside her.

She didn't look up.

She didn't need to.

She felt it.

Like a wall had been placed gently behind her back.

Like someone had quietly said: No more.

And behind that wall — stood Le.

Her mother had noticed.

Had acted.

Had protected.

That day, something shifted.

Not around her — but within her.

She still wore sunglasses.

Still sat a little apart.

Still studied at night to give her eyes peace.

But now, she walked home on time.

Because she no longer feared being seen.

Because when you know someone loves you enough to stand up for
you —

you begin to stand taller too.

That evening, Tien sat beside her mother in the soft hum of home.

Milu rested under the table, tail flicking gently,

as if he, too, felt the peace that had settled in the air.

Le was stitching a sleeve, glasses low on her nose.

Tien peeled a boiled egg, fingers slow, eyes thoughtful.

On the table sat a small pot of mung bean porridge with coconut milk, still warm.

It was a dish Le made when someone wasn't feeling well — soft, sweet, easy on the body.

The scent of pandan leaf mingled with the creamy steam,

wrapping around Tien like a blanket.

Le looked up and smiled.

"You should eat it before it cools. Good for your eyes."

Tien picked up her spoon and scooped a bit of the golden porridge.

It wasn't just food.

It was a quiet message.

You are cared for. You are seen.

Nothing dramatic had changed.

Her eyes still ached under light.

Her place in class remained at the front.

The sunglasses stayed on.

But something inside her had grown roots.

Her mother had seen her pain — and stood up.

Her teacher had spoken.

The cruel laughter had faded, even if not entirely.

She no longer had to fight alone.

Someone had lifted part of the weight.

No more whispers.

No more mud skipper jokes.

Just quiet respect.

Tien didn't need to lead a team.

She didn't need medals or boards with her name.

She just needed this:

149

A warm bowl of porridge.

A home where she was known.

And the slow, certain knowledge that even when life dims the light —

she still shines.

Chapter 20
The Singer of the House
And the Song That Carried Us

&

The phone rang just after dinner.

"Mum," Minh's voice crackled through the line,

"There's a singing competition at uni… tomorrow's the finale. I made it to the last round. Can you come?"

There was a pause.

"It's okay if you're busy with sewing," he added quickly.

Le held the phone close and turned to Tien.

"Tien, your brother's in a singing competition. Tomorrow is the finale."

From Minh's end came a distant shout:

"Can I come? Please! Please!"

Le smiled.

"We're coming."

By dawn, Le was in the kitchen.

She packed a small tin of salted fish, sticky rice, and a few treats Minh liked.

At the last moment, she added pickled radish and a couple of sweet bananas —

just in case he forgot to eat later.

Tien could hardly stay still.

She told every friend she passed,

"My brother's the singer tonight!"

The trip to the provincial centre was long.

First, a wooden boat that glided through morning mist,

then a bus rattling past rice fields and waving palms.

By late morning, they reached Minh's boarding house.

He was already waiting outside.

Beside him stood a tall girl with gentle eyes and a soft smile.

"Mum, this is Mai," Minh said shyly.

Tien stared wide-eyed.

"She's so pretty! Is she a model?"

Mai laughed and knelt beside her.

"No, sweetheart, I just like pretty shoes."

While Le unpacked the food and filled his cabinet with rice jars,

Mai took Tien by the hand and gave her a quick tour —

small rooms, narrow balconies, laundry lines fluttering in the wind.

Meanwhile, Le moved quietly in the shared kitchen.

She had brought fresh river fish from the village — small, sweet, and clean.

She deep-fried them until they were crisp and golden.

The smell drifted through the hallways,

drawing students from their rooms like moths to light.

Then she made the sauce — ginger, fish sauce, fresh chilli, and a hint of sugar.

Balanced. Fragrant. Irresistible.

Tien came running back, dragging Mai with her.

"Is lunch ready? I smelled the ginger from the end of the hallway!"

They sat cross-legged on the floor, sharing stories and hot, crackling fish.

It wasn't a banquet.

But it tasted like celebration.

As the sun dipped toward the horizon, Minh left to prepare backstage.

Mai stayed behind and led Le and Tien across the field,

where clusters of students were already gathering.

She scanned the crowd and smiled.

"We need a good spot," she said.

"And by that, I mean…"

She pointed to a tall tree near the courtyard's edge.

Its low, wide branches were strong enough for a small girl with a big heart.

Tien's eyes lit up.

Moments later, she was perched on a sturdy branch, legs swinging, face glowing.

From there, she could see everything.

One by one, students performed — songs of love, heartbreak, hope.

Some were nervous.

Some sang with wide grins.

Then Minh's name was called.

He stepped onto the stage —

not just her brother anymore, but a star.

He held the microphone with gentle ease.

His voice wasn't loud — but warm. Sweet.

Like water over stone.

Mid-song, his eyes found theirs — and he smiled.

His final note drifted into the dark like a thread of light —

and then the applause broke like rain.

When the results were announced, Minh's name was called as the champion.

The courtyard roared.

His classmates lifted him in the air, cheering.

And beneath the tree, Le's eyes filled with tears.

She didn't clap right away.

She just watched — heart full.

Tien, still on the branch, shouted,

"That's my brother!"

And no one could deny it.

The next morning, before the city stirred,

Tien half-woke to the sound of soft voices.

Le and Minh were speaking outside the kitchen.

"Minh… why Mai?" Le asked gently.

A pause.

"We love each other," Minh said.

"She's from our village. She's sweet. She's… everything.

And yes, she's wealthy — but not arrogant."

Le was quiet.

Then she said what hurt her to say:

"Minh, her mother will never accept a poor husband for her golden daughter."

Silence.

Not rejection. Just sorrow.

Le didn't want to break something so real.

But she had lived long enough to know what love sometimes couldn't fix.

On the bus ride home, Le said little.

She stared out the window, eyes far away.

Tien leaned her head on her mother's shoulder and whispered,

"You crying again?"

Le shook her head.

Tien grinned.

"Must be onions."

Le smiled.

But something heavy lingered behind her eyes.

After a while, she turned to Tien.

"Your brother… he eats too little."

Tien blinked.

"What do you mean?"

"When I arranged his cabinet, I found more salted fish.

Poor ones. Old soya cheese.

He's saving money — eating cheap, salty things."

Tien fell quiet.

Then she nodded firmly.

"We'll visit him more often, Mum.

We'll bring better food next time. Good food."

Le didn't reply right away.

She just reached over and held her daughter's hand.

And as the road stretched out before them,

Tien leaned closer — vowing, in the quiet way only a child can, to protect the one who sang like the stars

and ate like he didn't matter.

She would carry his name,

his hunger,

his light —

in her heart, always.

Chapter 21
The Taste of Memory
And the Rice Gathered After the Harvest

&

That night, after they returned home, the house was quiet.

No food was ready.

Le opened the pantry and unwrapped a salted fish — just one.

She sliced it gently and dropped it into a hot pan with sugar, vinegar, garlic, and chilli.

The sauce sizzled — sharp and fragrant.

Tien rinsed the rice, sliced cucumber into thin rounds.

By the time the fish turned golden and crisp,

the rice had steamed soft and white.

Dinner was simple.

A white bowl of rice.

Fresh green cucumber.

And sweet and sour salted fish — glistening, red-brown, crackling with heat.

Tien took one bite and smiled.

"Mum," she said softly,

"I think Brother really loves your salted fish — not just because it's cheap… but because it's yours."

Le laughed gently, but her eyes turned distant.

She looked at the rice, then began:

"Before you were born, Minh was about ten.

His father had already left. Things were hard."

She paused.

"One night, Minh came back from Grandma's house during dinner.

He didn't say much. Just looked at me and said —

'Mum, I'm craving white rice.'"

Tien sat very still.

Le's voice softened.

"It felt like a knife.

I couldn't sleep that night.

I kept thinking — I'm a terrible mother.

I can't even give my son white rice."

"But Minh…" she smiled faintly,

"Minh was strong."

"When harvest time came, he'd run to the fields after school.

He waited until the farmers finished,

then asked to gather what was left."

"One day, he came home with a small bag of broken rice.

He smashed it by hand to remove the husk.

Most of it was cracked — but he held it like treasure and said,

'Mum, how long will this last?'"

"He wanted to plan.

To make sure we always had rice.

He said, 'We'll have rice from now on.'"

Tien didn't speak.

Her chest ached with love.

Le added quietly,

"That night, we had rice, boiled vegetables,

and salt with chilli in lemon juice.

But Minh ate like it was a feast."

Le smiled and continued:

"I still remember — as the pot of rice began to bubble,

he kept coming into the kitchen just to smell it.

His face lit up like it was Tet.

He leaned close to the steam and said,

'Mum, white rice smells so good.'"

Now, Tien understood.

The taste of salted fish.

The love behind it.

The quiet, wordless bond between her mother and her brother.

It wasn't just food.

It was forged in hunger,

in sacrifice,

and in a promise:

We won't give up.

She took another bite. Slowly.

To honour the boy who once gathered broken rice from the dust —

so they would never go without again.

Chapter 22
Wired with Light
And the Power She Chose to Hold

Ⴛ

The house crackled more often now —

not with joy, but with faulty switches and buzzing bulbs.

The wiring was tired.

So was Le.

When things broke, Le walked gently to the neighbour's house.

"Can you help me change a bulb?" she'd ask.

Sometimes they helped.

Sometimes they didn't.

One day, Tien heard the shout —

not from her mother, but from the neighbour.

Disrespect, loud enough to echo through the alley.

Le returned, shoulders small.

"Sometimes you must bow your head to get help," she said softly.

Tien stared at the flickering light.

Not forever, she thought.

The next day, she came home from school with purpose.

"Mum, I want to take the career classes early — this year."

Le looked up.

"What's available?"

"Farming or electric."

"Then choose farming. It's easier."

Tien shook her head.

"Our house has no man," She said – but her voice didn't tremble

"If I learn electric, no one will shout at you again."

Le looked at her daughter — small, quiet, but filled with light —

and nodded.

Tien joined the class.

The only girl.

"Electric's for boys," someone muttered.

She didn't respond.

Mr Bao, the teacher, knew her mother.

He'd seen Le carry broken plugs to neighbours who rolled their eyes.

"Electricity isn't a toy," he told her.

"If you don't respect it, it doesn't forgive."

She nodded. She studied.

She passed.

With her certificate tucked in her schoolbag,

she walked home —

now as her mother's electrician.

Her chance came quickly.

During English class, the tape player died.

"Fuse again," the teacher sighed.

The class cheered.

"We can go home!"

Tien raised her hand.

"I can fix it."

The teacher blinked.

"Really?"

"I passed the test."

She fixed it in minutes.

The radio clicked back on.

English voices filled the room.

Some classmates groaned.

"Tien! We could've gone home!"

She smiled.

She wasn't trying to impress anyone.

She was just doing what needed to be done.

At home, she used the same plastic stool.

Replaced the hallway fuse.

Fixed the kitchen switch.

Le watched from the doorway, eyes glassy.

"You've grown up," she said.

"You've given me peace."

Then, the neighbour's mother knocked.

"Our fuse blew. Can you help?"

Tien went without hesitation.

She did it swiftly.

That evening, the man who once shouted at Le came to their door.

"Thanks… and sorry. For before."

Tien didn't say it was okay.

She just nodded.

She had already answered — with her hands.

And with each wire,

she rewrote the story of her home.

No longer waiting in the dark.

Chapter 23
The Rain Above and the Thread Below
And the Love That Didn't Leave

&

The doctor said the kidney stones were back.

This time, the pain was sharper.

The medicine helped —

but the sewing slowed.

Le tried to pretend it was fine.

But each day, her back hunched sooner over the table.

Her stitches grew slower.

So Tien stepped in again.

Cooking. Cleaning.

Listening for the rhythm of the machine.

And when friends came, asking her to come play or study,

her voice stayed calm:

"I can't today. I need to take care of Mum."

It became her usual answer.

She didn't mind the chores.

She minded the rain.

When the sky cracked open and the roof began to leak,

she knew she wouldn't sleep much.

A plastic sheet hung over their bed, catching the falling water.

But when it rained hard, the water pooled and sagged,

threatening to collapse.

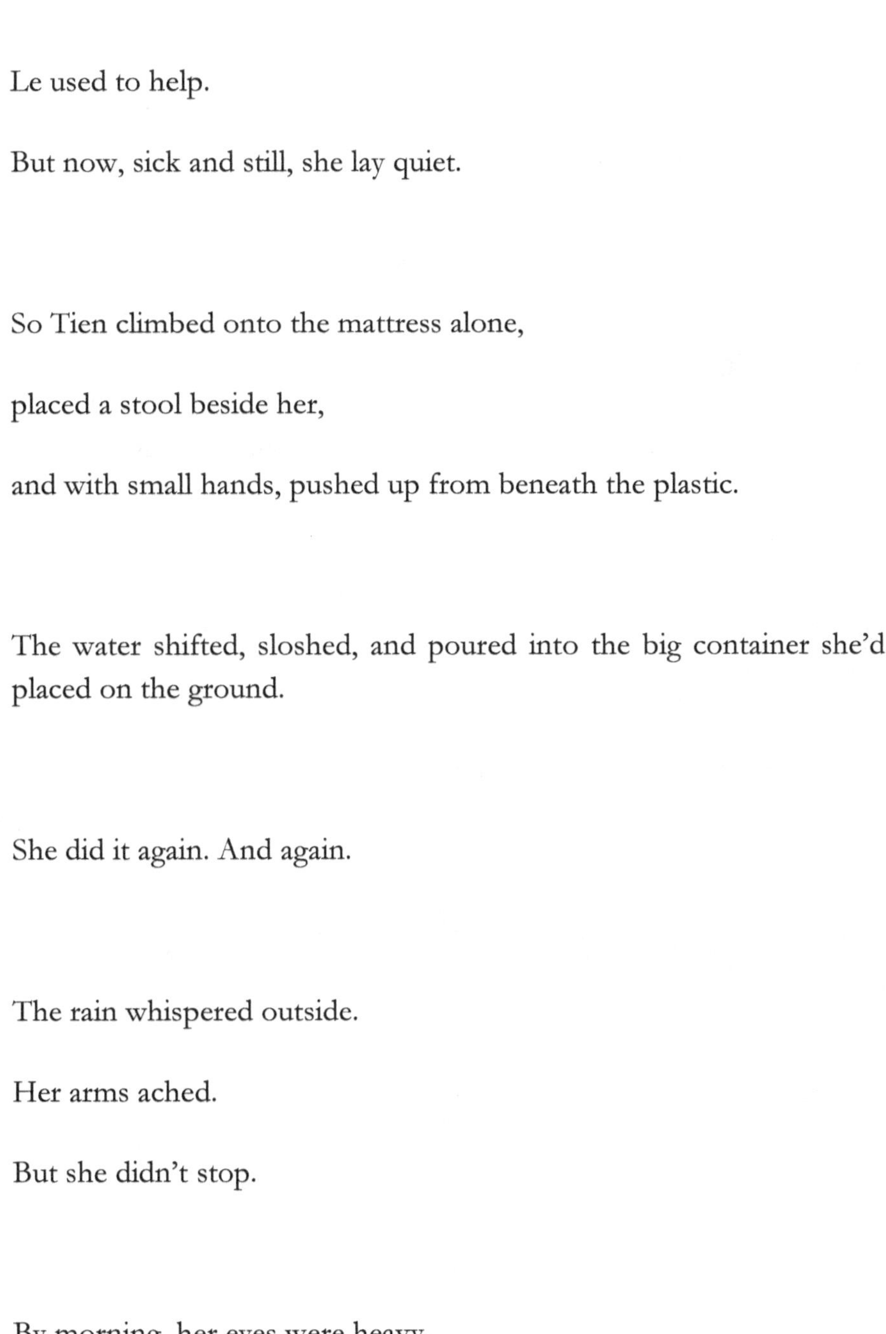

Le used to help.

But now, sick and still, she lay quiet.

So Tien climbed onto the mattress alone,

placed a stool beside her,

and with small hands, pushed up from beneath the plastic.

The water shifted, sloshed, and poured into the big container she'd placed on the ground.

She did it again. And again.

The rain whispered outside.

Her arms ached.

But she didn't stop.

By morning, her eyes were heavy.

But the house was dry.

One afternoon, while Le was stitching a button onto a purple áo dài, the phone rang.

She frowned, needle still in hand.

"Tien, dear, can you pick up for me? Put it on speaker, please."

Tien pressed the button.

A woman's voice floated through the room — elegant, but cold.

"Hi Le, how are you? Do you know where your son is?"

Le paused.

"Now? He's gone to another province for his final practice.

He'll be back in a few days. Why?"

But in her heart, she already knew.

When Mai's mother called, it was never for small talk.

It was about Minh.

About Mai.

And the love Le had hoped had faded —

especially after news that Mai was soon to marry a foreign man.

The voice on the phone didn't tremble,

but there was steel beneath it.

"Mai is going to marry a foreign man. The wedding is tomorrow."

Le's needle paused mid-air.

"Oh, congratulations," she said politely.

A pause.

"But… she disappeared yesterday. No one can find her. The groom is here, waiting."

Le's heart began to pound.

Now she understood.

Mai's mother hadn't called to share joy —

she had called to reclaim what she believed was stolen.

"So you think Mai is with Minh?" Le asked softly.

"Not that I think, Le. I know," the woman said.

"If you can find out Minh's address in Cần Thơ, give it to me.

The wedding needs the bride tomorrow.

If not, it will be a shame on my family.

You're a mother — you must understand."

Le looked toward the sewing machine.

The fabric lay still.

Her hands trembled — barely.

"Yes, I know how it feels," she replied quietly.

"But I also know my son.

Minh would never seduce your daughter.

He's never been that kind of man."

"Mai left home to see Minh, she has been crying the whole week" the woman said again,

her voice tightening near a cry.

Le's chest ached — for the young love.

For the mother's desperation.

For her own fear of what might come next.

She answered calmly:

"If I know where they are, I'll tell you.

I'll call Minh's friends now."

She ended the call, slowly set down the phone,

and sat in silence for a moment.

She didn't wait long.

Not even an hour later, the phone rang again.

It was Minh.

"Mum," he said, voice low and hurried,

"Can you wire me some money — right now?"

He didn't explain why. But he didn't need to.

Le closed her eyes, breathing in the silence.

Then she said gently:

"I'll go to town and send it to you after this call.

But Minh — tell Mai to come home.

Her wedding is tomorrow.

Please."

A pause.

She didn't wait for answers.

She trusted her words would be enough.

Tien didn't know the full story, but in her bones, she sensed it:

Something sacred had been broken —

By the fear of what people might say.

By the weight of gold and status dressed as tradition.

And by the quiet breaking of two hearts that deserved gentleness.

The next day, the wedding had its bride.

Mai returned.

No stories were told.

No explanations were needed.

Only this:

Minh, Mai, and Le had done what was necessary.

Not for pride.

Not for fear.

But because they each carried love in their own way —

and sometimes, love means letting go without asking why.

That evening, after the wedding was done and the day turned to dusk,

Le returned home and hung her jacket by the door.

The sewing machine sat silent.

The rice cooker was still warm.

Tien met her at the table with two bowls and a small teapot.

The gentle aroma of jasmine tea drifted through the air —

sweet, floral, comforting.

Le noticed the little porcelain cup already waiting for her,

steam rising gently in the quiet room.

"Did the wedding go okay?" Tien asked softly.

Le nodded, eyes tired but kind.

"Yes. It had its bride. Mai walked like a daughter returning from battle, not a bride stepping into joy, don't tell your brother"

Tien didn't ask more.

She could feel the weight in her mother's shoulders —

love held back, pride swallowed,

and a son silently protected.

Le sat down and cupped the tea in her hands.

The scent wrapped around her like a memory.

She took a slow sip and looked toward her daughter.

"Sometimes we do what we must —

not because it's easy,

but because we know what it means to be a mother."

Tien watched her closely,

the lamplight reflecting in the tea between them.

And in that moment,

she understood something more about love:

It wasn't loud.

It didn't boast.

It simply stayed.

That night, after the tea had cooled and Tien had gone to bed,

Le picked up the phone once more.

She didn't know what words to use, so she kept it simple.

"Minh, come home this weekend."

A pause.

"I'll make bánh xèo. Your favourite."

She didn't say she knew he was hurting.

She didn't mention the wedding, or Mai,

or the silence in his voice when he asked for money.

She just offered what she could.

A warm meal.

A familiar taste.

And a mother's presence.

And that was how she held the thread —

beneath the storm, beneath the silence —

where only love remained.

~

Years later, when the world mocked Minh for how fiercely he guarded his wife — when he refused to let her be shamed, questioned, or diminished — Tien remembered this moment.

He had once lost someone to the gods of reputation and fortune.

He would never let it happen again.

192

Chapter 24
The Edge of Bánh Xèo
(Vietnamese Crispy Sizzling Crepes)
And the Healing Hidden in Crisp Edges

৸

Minh returned home that weekend — silent, heart-bruised.

He didn't say a word.

But Tien knew.

So did Le.

The same three plastic chairs waited beneath the kumquat tree in the front yard —

weathered by sun, softened by time.

No questions were asked.

Just three people.

Three cups of tea.

One tree blooming quietly in their corner of the world.

Minh sat down slowly,

as if the weight in his chest had finally brought him to stillness.

Le poured the tea without a word.

Tien passed him the cup.

Maybe he felt guilty for asking for money.

Maybe the empty boarding house — once filled with Mai's laughter —
had become unbearable.

Or maybe he simply longed for shelter.

Le and Tien soon moved to the kitchen.

Rice flour. Coconut milk. Sizzling pans.

The scent of turmeric and pork filled the air.

While they cooked, Minh carried the laundry basket to the washbasin outside.

It had always been his job.

He didn't need to be told.

He just did it.

Tien watched from the doorway, a quiet grin on her face.

If he hadn't come, she would've had to do it.

Between them, there was no talk of sorrow or breakups.

Only the familiar rhythm of home.

A silent promise shared since childhood:

Lighten Mum's load. Together.

And that morning, as the edges of the bánh xèo crackled golden in the pan,

the air filled with something softer than sadness —

a kind of healing that didn't need words.

Just food.

Warmth.

Presence.

The only task Tien never dared take on was bánh xèo.

It needed a quick wrist and perfect timing —

the kind of movement that lived only in Le's hands.

Still, she stayed near the stove as Le fried the crepes,

waiting like a child who already knew the reward.

When one bánh xèo finished sizzling, Le set it aside to cool.

That was Tien's moment.

She'd sneak a little piece off the edge —

the crispy lace was her favourite part.

Better than any chip in the village.

By noon, lunch was ready.

Le placed a plate of golden bánh xèo on the table

beside a bowl of sweet and sour fish sauce.

Beside it was a mountain of fresh greens —

mustard cabbage, lettuce, mint, Vietnamese mint, and fish mint.

Everything smelled like home.

Minh and Tien sat down.

Then all three of them paused.

They looked at the bánh xèo.

Something was off.

The crepes were there…

but none had their crispy edges.

Le narrowed her eyes.

Minh tilted his head.

Then both turned to Tien — who smiled her brightest, widest grin.

Le let out a laugh.

"Tien! You edge thief!"

Minh joined in.

"No wonder it smelled so good before lunch — you already had half of it!"

Tien shrugged, laughing.

"You were slow. I got hungry."

The table filled with lightness again.

No one asked Minh about the wedding.

No one said the word Mai.

They just wrapped their bánh xèo with herbs,

dipped it in sauce,

and ate like it was the only thing that mattered.

And in that quiet, golden lunch,

they found what they needed —

not answers,

not closure,

just warmth,

greens,

laughter…

and the crisp edge of something whole again.

Chapter 25
The Golden Sip
And the Prize She Didn't Have to Earn

৪৯

Year 9 was the year of quiet exams for most.

But for Tien, it was the year of a call.

"Tien, join the English team."

"You'd be perfect for Chemistry."

"What about Maths?"

Each teacher saw promise in her —

something rare in their small village school.

Mrs Dan, her English teacher, smiled as she handed over a form.

"You speak clearly, and your writing sings.

The English team would be lucky to have you."

Tien smiled, thanked her softly,

but in the end, chose Physics.

Mrs Dan's smile faltered.

Then she gently touched Tien's shoulder.

"Give it your best, Tien. I'm proud of you either way."

Tien nodded, heart steady.

She trained with the school's top four.

Her eyes no longer wept under light.

Her hands moved swiftly across pages.

She was focused. Determined.

The first round arrived: town level.

The competition was fierce.

Tien's score: 10 out of 20.

Just enough to pass.

Not enough to shine.

Her teacher smiled —

but his eyes dropped.

Le said gently,

"You passed. That's good enough."

But it didn't feel good enough.

Tien stayed up late,

reworking mistakes, pencil in hand, eyes half-shut over formulas.

Each number, each symbol — a step towards proving she belonged.

Her desk became her bed.

Milu, ever loyal, curled beside her feet.

Le noticed.

She didn't scold.

She brought supper.

Warm tea.

Quiet presence.

Until one night, a new scent filled the house —

sweet, earthy, healing.

Tien followed it to the kitchen.

Jujube.

Lotus seed.

Longan.

And something else — soft and ancient —

a root she couldn't name.

A golden tonic simmered on the stove, gentle as prayer.

Le handed her a bowl.

"Have a sip."

The warmth seeped into her bones.

The scent wrapped her like a lullaby.

And for the first time in weeks, the weight eased —

not because of results,

but because of love.

"Thank you, Mum," Tien whispered.

Le smoothed her daughter's hair.

"Don't chase after recognition," she said.

"I'm already proud.

I love you — whether you win or not."

And in that quiet bowl of gold,

Tien tasted something better than achievement —

a mother's pride,

a healing sip,

and the kind of love

that never kept score.

Chapter 26
The Province Seat
And the Score No One Expected

&

The morning of the province competition came softly.

No loud alarms.

No rush.

Just the pale blue of early light brushing across the walls of their small house.

Tien had been awake before the sun.

Not studying.

Just sitting.

Her notebooks were closed.

Her pencils lined up neatly on the table.

Milu lay curled at her feet, watching without words.

For once, the house was quiet —

not from exhaustion,

but from readiness.

Le entered the kitchen, cardigan wrapped around her, hair still tied from sleep.

She didn't say good luck.

She didn't give instructions.

She simply placed a small rice cake and a flask of warm pandan tea beside Tien's hand.

Without looking at her daughter, she said,

"You've done all you can."

Tien nodded.

She patted Milu gently, stood, straightened her uniform,

and slipped her bag over her shoulder.

Outside, the morning mist clung low to the road.

She walked slowly — not from fear,

but from the weight of what she carried.

Not just her notes.

But her school's hope.

Mrs Dan's encouragement.

Her teacher's silence.

Her mother's belief.

And something deeper — her own quiet worth.

She whispered as she walked,

"God, I've done my part. I leave the rest to you."

The bus ride to the province was long, but quiet.

Tien sat by the window, her breath soft against the glass.

Beside her, her teammates chatted, whispered last-minute equations.

But her mind lingered on her Physics teacher's words:

"I don't have much hope in you. Town — 10 out of 20.

How can you survive the province?"

He hadn't meant to be cruel.

Tien knew that.

His voice had been sharp —

but beneath it was disappointment, wrapped in worry.

She didn't feel angry.

She didn't feel sad.

She just felt… light.

No one expects me to succeed. She thought.

No more burden now,

And strangely, that gave her peace.

The exam hall was vast. Quiet. Cool.

Tien sharpened her pencil once.

Then again — until it felt just right.

When the papers were handed out,

she scanned the questions slowly.

Her heartbeat stayed even.

She didn't rush.

She didn't panic.

She simply answered.

The bell rang.

It was over.

Afterwards, the teacher gathered the team in a quiet room.

He asked for their answers — question by question.

Then came the final one — the hardest.

The one meant to separate top scores from the rest.

Tien gave her answer calmly.

The teacher's eyes narrowed.

"Wrong," he said.

That was all.

Her classmate heard it.

He didn't say much in the moment.

But the moment didn't stay quiet.

The next day, back at school,

the whispers started before she entered the room.

"Tien failed again."

"She embarrassed the teacher."

"Mocked our class. Twice."

"Why did she even go to the province?"

Tien stood at the doorway.

Her hand tightened around her bag.

She had studied.

She had walked in with no armour.

She had walked out with no complaint.

But now, their whispers felt like hands —

pushing her back out of the room.

The day the results came, the sky was clear.

Tien walked to school with her usual calm,

unaware that the world was already shifting.

Le had left early for the village market.

Tien stepped through the school gate,

ready for another ordinary day.

Then —

"Tien! Tien! Stop!"

She turned.

Her Physics teacher was running across the courtyard, breathless.

"You got 19 out of 20!" he blurted.

"I was wrong. Your answer — it was right. The only correct one!"

Tien blinked, stunned.

"The second-highest score was 10.

You didn't just pass, Tien…

You set a new record for this school."

Her hands flew to her mouth.

"I… I don't know what to say — thank you, sir!

It's all thanks to your teaching!"

He smiled.

"You've made this school proud.

Go tell your class."

When she walked into the classroom, the noise exploded.

"Congratulations, Tien!"

"Top in the whole province!"

Even the voices that once whispered now clapped for her.

She smiled, humbled.

Not to prove anything.

Just grateful that her quiet fire had finally been seen.

That afternoon, as soon as class ended, she ran —

past the gate, down the road, faster than ever.

Halfway home, she saw Milu trotting ahead.

"Milu!" she laughed, chasing after him,

feet pounding joy into the dust.

She burst through the front door, shouting:

"Mum! I did it!"

Le came running from the kitchen, apron on, wooden spoon in hand.

"I already know!" she beamed.

"Your English teacher told me at the market!

Mrs Dan — she was so proud. So am I."

Tien threw her arms around her mother,

breathless, laughing, happy.

In the kitchen, Le pulled her in.

"Sit down. Don't touch anything — today, you're just the guest."

The pot on the stove was already bubbling.

"What is it?" Tien asked.

"Chicken congee. With lots of pepper.

And your favourite — banana tree salad with herbs and chilli."

It wasn't a fancy feast.

It didn't need to be.

It was the kind of food that said:

I see you.

I'm proud of you.

I've been waiting to celebrate you.

Le ladled the congee into a bowl and placed the salad beside it —

the banana stem crisp, glistening with lime juice and roasted peanut.

Tien took the first bite slowly.

The warmth sank into her bones.

The sharp crunch lifted the flavour

like sunlight on water.

She didn't say a word.

But her eyes filled again —

not from exhaustion this time,

but from joy.

Chapter 27
The Song Beneath the Window
And the Keys That Welcomed Joy

&

The morning after her province victory, the world glowed.

The sun poured through the window in golden streaks.

The fan hummed softly.

And for once, there were no exams waiting on the table.

Tien stretched, rubbed her eyes, and shuffled into the kitchen.

Le handed her a small folded note — crisp bills tucked inside.

"Here," she smiled.

"Treat yourself to any breakfast you like."

Tien's hair was still a little wild, but her steps were light.

She knew exactly where she was going.

At the bánh mì stall by the river,

the smell of fresh bread and coriander drifted in the morning breeze.

Tien smiled at the woman behind the cart.

"My usual, please."

"Coming right up," the woman said, wrapping the warm roll with care.

Tien took her seat beside the river,

steam rising from the bread,

sun warming her shoulders.

There were no tests today.
No weight to carry.

Just sunshine, bánh mì,

and the quiet joy of being victorious.

That evening, back home, she stepped through the door expecting nothing.

But in the centre of the living room sat a new keyboard.

Bigger than her old one.

Second-hand, but sturdy.

The keys still glossy, waiting.

Le peeked from the kitchen.

"It's not expensive…

But it has more keys — you can play more now."

Tien froze.

Ran her fingers along the edge.

"Mum… thank you."

That night, she played.

No teacher. No sheet music.

Just memory.

Her fingers remembered what her heart already knew.

Neighbours slowed their steps.

Children paused by the fence.

Someone pulled out a stool to listen.

Tien didn't play to impress.

She played to remember.

And beneath her fingertips,

light filled the street.

On warmer evenings, she returned to the keyboard like a diary.

No chords. No pedals.

Just her and the treble clef.

Sometimes Le would pause from sewing.

"That one reminds me of the old days," she'd say.

Tien smiled, and played on.

One night, Le whispered from her chair:

"I wish I had more money.

If you were born in a wealthy family,

you'd shine so bright, the world would have to look."

Tien stopped.

"I love what I have now, Mum.

This keyboard is the best gift ever."

It was true.

The joy she felt when playing — the spark of music — began with the small toy keyboard

from a father who, despite the distance,

had unknowingly planted a seed that would never stop growing.

One evening, she played something light.

Unscripted. Joyful.

A small voice called out:

"Play the happy one again!"

Three children crouched near the steps.

Tien laughed shyly — and played it again.

More children came.

That night, her music didn't just fill the house.

It spilled into the street.

The keyboard never asked her to be perfect.

It simply welcomed her –

again and again.

Chapter 28
The Day She Was Seen
And the Stage That Reached Home

The scholarship was real.

A national award —

For Talented Female Students of Vietnam.

Tien had won.

Out of thousands — maybe tens of thousands.

Her name was listed.

The award would be presented live — on television.

In another province.

On a real stage.

But Le couldn't come.

The cost of travel was too much.

The sewing orders too many.

The money too little.

Tien understood.

That morning, she packed quietly.

Three other girls from her region gathered at the province hall.

Each arrived with parents —

mothers in pressed áo dài,

fathers with cameras and bouquets.

Tien came alone.

She wore her school uniform and held her name card.

No flowers.

No camera.

No hand to hold.

But she remembered what Le had said before she left:

"I'll see you on TV — with the whole neighbourhood."

Back home, Le had stopped sewing.

She cleaned the floor, wiped the television screen,

and placed extra chairs in the small living room.

She told everyone:

"Tien will be on television – my daughter."

And they came.

Neighbours. Aunties. Children.

All crowding into the little house

to watch the girl from their alley

walk across a stage meant for cities and lights.

Tien stood under those lights,

blinked at the crowd,

and smiled.

She knew her mother was watching.

And that was enough.

She didn't walk the stage alone.
She carried her whole street with her.

Chapter 29
The Broken Rice Year
And the Bitterness She Chose Not to Keep

 है

When the letter came, Le didn't cry.

She held it close, then pressed it gently into Tien's hands.

"You've been accepted," she said.

"Top high school in the town. Selective class. I'm proud of you."

Tien nodded — but inside, her chest ached.

It meant leaving her mother.

It meant starting again.

The town school was not like her village one.

It was bigger. Louder.

And crueller.

Tien wore glasses. She came from a poor background.

And worst of all — her brother was a teacher at the school.

So when she earned praise, they said it was because of him.

The rich students laughed in corners.

She heard whispers when she passed.

She was quiet, so they mistook that for weakness.

Her only friend was Oanh —

a girl from her old school who came to the new one with her.

One soul in a sea of polished uniforms and rehearsed lies.

They sat together when they could.

They didn't talk much—but they didn't have to.

Sometimes just walking side by side was enough.

Tien didn't fight back.

She studied. Hard.

Stayed up when others slept.

Reread books when her eyes hurt.

And by the second half of Year 10, she rose to the top.

Even the bullies went silent.

By Year 11, they asked for help with homework.

She gave it.

Not out of fear — but because she wouldn't let bitterness change her.

Minh got married that year.

His wife, Lan, was also a teacher at the school.

At first, Tien hoped it meant family would grow stronger.

But Lan didn't hide her dislike.

Tien thought about moving out more than once.

But living alone meant higher costs — and a quiet complication.

Both Minh and Lan were teachers at the same school.

Minh had once told Le,

"If she moves out, people will talk. It won't look good for us."

So Tien stayed.

Not because she lacked strength.

But because she didn't want to bring trouble

to the one who had once carried her on his shoulders.

Lan didn't like Le.

She didn't like Tien.

And now, living together in Minh's house, it became clear.

Tien would come home late from school and find the food nearly gone

what remained was bad-smelling rice, wilted soup, and fatty meat

she had to force herself to eat.

She never complained. She still paid Lan food money every month.

But sometimes, when the house fell quiet

and Lan's footsteps echoed down the hall,

Tien would pause mid-bite —

feeling more unwelcome than hungry.

She thought of Le.

Of how her mother had endured insults, cold shoulders, long silences

from those who felt entitled to more.

Tien could feel that same bitterness rising in her.

But she pushed it down.

Tien didn't want to carry that kind of weight.

"I will not pass this pain forward," she told herself.

"I will not let it shape me."

When the food no longer fed her,

she quietly walked to a bánh mì shop nearby.

Then one day, she wandered into a small restaurant

tucked between two old buildings.

They served cơm tấm — broken rice with grilled pork and shredded
pork skin.

And she stayed.

Day after day, for a full year.

The owner noticed.

She noticed Tien's quiet hunger, her worn-out uniform, her patience.

Her son had autism.

Tien treated him with gentleness. Never stared. Never flinched.

One afternoon, the woman brought a small plate from her own kitchen.

"You can't eat that one dish forever," she said.

"Try this fried fish. It's good."

Tien smiled, bowed her head, and whispered:

"Thank you."

It was the only kindness she'd tasted that week.

~

There's a reason broken rice tastes different.

It was once whole — but broken in the milling.

In the same way, some years feel like that.

Shattered by harsh hands. Crushed by unseen weight.

But those who endure don't lose their worth.

Broken rice still nourishes.

And sometimes, in its humble form,

it feeds the soul more than any perfect grain ever could.

Tien's year wasn't defined by cruelty —

but by what she chose to keep.

Chapter 30
The Bowl Beside Her Bed
And the Love That Arrived in Silence

&

Year 12 was a race without a finish line.

Tien studied harder than ever. Exams loomed. Her dreams narrowed.

But even the small support she once had began to slip away.

Lan no longer let Minh help.

"Teach someone else's sister," she said gently, with a finality that didn't invite discussion.

Tien didn't protest. She quietly found another tutor.

It meant more riding. Less food. More silence.

The bad dreams returned — shadows, whispers, voices from nowhere.

One night, she dreamt of bloody hands placing books on her desk, the stumps still dripping.

She woke in a sweat.

Le told her to burn incense. To pray.

Tien did. But the dreams didn't stop.

Even the house began to pull away from her.

One day, she came home and noticed the living room TV was gone — moved into Minh and Lan's bedroom.

No more news. No more music. No more comfort. Just quiet.

Another day, she found her kettle dented — like something heavy had struck it.

Lan and Minh's kettle sat untouched on the other shelf.

It's not leaking, Tien told herself. *It just looks strange. I can keep using it.*

Her small radio, once her favourite companion, became another silence.

She used it each night for English lessons — soft, steady voices guiding her through difficult grammar.

But Lan complained

And so, even the radio was quiet.

The last comfort was gone.

Then came the accident.

Le had saved up for an old motorbike to make things easier.

Tien offered to ride it — with Le behind her. She wanted to be helpful.

Something went wrong on the road.

They fell.

Le escaped with only scrapes.

But Tien's left knee swelled badly.

The doctor said some tendons were torn.

It would take time to heal.

She couldn't bend it — not enough to ride her bike to school.

Minh helped at first.

Each morning, he took her to school on his motorbike, and brought her home.

But every evening, Tien heard the voices behind the door.

Lan's complaints. Tension that filled the air like smoke.

One night, Tien said to Minh,

"You don't have to take me anymore. I can ride by myself."

Minh looked at her, concerned, but didn't argue.

And the house fell quiet again.

Except for Tien, who now rode her bicycle each morning — leg stiff, pain sharp.

She winced with every push of the pedal.

But said nothing.

The hardest part was the bridge near her school.

The slope was too steep for her swollen knee.

Every morning, she had to jump off her bike at the foot of it, limping alongside it to the top — legs aching, breath short, hands gripping the handlebars.

Some days, she reached the top and wanted to stay there.

She pulled her hat low over her face — just enough to hide.

She didn't want other teachers to recognise her. To talk. To mock her brother.

From up there, the town looked quieter.

The river moved slowly below — brown and wide, dotted with fishing boats that looked like sleeping birds.

Morning light spilled through the clouds, golden, like a light from heaven.

And for a moment, it was beautiful.

Tien closed her eyes.

The river breeze stirred her hair, brushed her face, and carried with it the scent of water and distant reeds.

For a moment, it brought her back to her riverside village –

and it was good.

She took a long, steady breath.

Then got back on the bike —

and rode to school.

One morning, she opened her schoolbag. Her food money was missing.

She asked Minh quietly. He handed her a few notes, said nothing.

Later, she called Le.

"Can you bring me some cash tomorrow? I'll stretch it."

That night, the fever came.

Burning behind her eyes.

Her body ached.

Her throat felt raw.

She whispered through the wall.

"Minh… I've got a fever."

No reply.

"Lan…"

Still silence.

She dragged herself to the dented kettle. There was a little warm water left.

She sipped it on the kitchen floor, hands trembling.

Just let me reach morning, she prayed.

Let me see Mum.

And somehow — she did.

When morning came, Le stepped into the room and saw her daughter curled near the edge of her bed, as if she had tried to get up before her mother came in.

She rushed to her, voice breaking.

"Why didn't anyone help you?"

Tien touched her mother's hand.

"Don't say anything, Mum. Please."

Le didn't argue.

She wiped her forehead, took her to the doctor.

And once they returned home, she moved to the kitchen.

She sliced ginger. Cleaned a small piece of fish.

Simmered rice in a pot.

The scent of pepper and ginger wrapped around the house like an embrace.

When the congee was ready, Le brought a bowl to Tien's bedside.

"Eat a little," she whispered.

"It'll help you sweat it out."

Tien took a spoonful.

The warmth soothed her throat.

Her eyes filled — not from fever, but tenderness.

"Thank you," she said.

And meant it.

For the soup.

For her mother's silence.

For still being held — when everything else had let go.

In that small warmth,

the night didn't feel quite so cruel.

252

Chapter 31
The One-Eye Champion
And the Light They Couldn't Take

❧

It began with a blur.

Just a dull patch in her left eye —

harmless at first, like a shadow on glass.

But the blur grew.

It blocked out the blackboard.

Dimmed street signs she used to read with ease.

Le took her to the big city eye hospital.

They sat for hours as nurses called names and ran tests.

When the doctor returned,

he asked Le to wait outside.

Tien sat across from him —

the white coat between them,

his expression too gentle to be casual.

"You have a parasite infection," he said softly.

"It's already done damage. I'm very sorry —

but the vision in your left eye is gone.

Permanently."

She froze.

The words didn't feel real.

But she steadied her voice.

"Please, don't tell my mum."

The doctor looked at her kindly, but firmly.

"I'm sorry. You're under eighteen.

I have to inform your guardian."

On the bus ride home, neither of them said much.

Le stared out the window.

Tien watched the blur of trees

with the one eye that still saw clearly.

Then her mother whispered, barely a breath:

"I'm sorry… if we had more money…

if we had checked your eyes earlier, maybe…"

Tien reached for her hand.

"No, Mum. It's not your fault.

I didn't tell you.

I knew the tests would be expensive,

so I pretended it was fine."

Le wiped her tears in silence.

But Tien added, stronger now:

"The other eye is strong.

I can still see the world.

I'll study harder.

I'll stay top of the class."

That night, Le asked Tien quietly:

"Do you still want to lead your teams at school? You don't have to."

Tien shook her head.

"I still have one good eye.

I can still help my friends."

And she did —

Still the team leader for English, Physics, and Biology.

Still studying late.

Still helping others revise.

Still holding light where she could.

That year, she was awarded the town's highest student scholarship —

Student of the Year.

Her name was printed on the school board beside three others.

She was the only girl.

The students cheered.

Her teachers praised her.

It felt like the reward after all the storm.

~

Some lights don't shine from a stage —

they flicker quietly behind closed doors,

or burn steady beneath a bandage and a brave smile.

Tien never sought applause.

But when it came, it found her still holding on —

to faith, to kindness, to the part of herself that kept seeing

even with one eye closed.

Chapter 32
The Name That Disappeared
And the Strength That Stayed

❧

The final ceremony came with banners and bright lights.

Tien sat in her chair — back straight, uniform pressed.

But her name was never called.

She watched as others walked up to the stage.

The applause rang out.

The flowers were handed over.

Whispers began to ripple through the crowd:

"She was on the list."

"Why wasn't her name announced?"

Later, she found out.

The teacher responsible for submitting the final list had quietly crossed out her name.

No warning.

No reason.

No apology.

Minh called Le that afternoon,

while Tien was still riding home.

He had heard from a colleague what had happened —

that Tien's name had been removed.

Not lost.

Not forgotten.

Removed.

Le didn't cry.

She didn't call Tien.

She simply set the table and made dinner.

Her hands steady as ever.

Tien stopped just outside the front gate.

She stared at the peeling paint,

the small fence,

the flickering light in the window.

That morning, she had promised her mum:

"I'll come back with the scholarship."

Now she had to walk in with empty hands.

She took a breath and stepped inside.

Le was waiting with dinner on the table —

a simple stir-fry of green beans with thin slices of pork, still steaming.

Beside it, soy sauce with red chilli. Their usual.

She didn't ask what happened.

She simply said:

"Come eat, darling."

Tien sat down.

The meal was quiet.

The dipping sauce had the right heat.

The beans still held their crunch.

The tears came later, in silence.

But even with one eye,

she saw it clearly:

They could take her name.

But not her light.

Her name didn't echo through the speakers.

But her strength spoke louder than any microphone.

That was the last day of high school.

And Tien came home with Le — to their house.

The next morning, Le found her awake early,

sitting at the table beside the kumquat tree.

She brought out two cups of tea and sat next to her.

She handed one to Tien and teased,

"Sitting here and no tea? Did you miss something?"

Tien smiled faintly but said nothing.

Le noticed her quiet.

She pointed gently to the sky.

"See that?"

"Yes, Mum. That's my high school in town."

"Every afternoon when the sun was about to set,

I'd come out here, sit on this chair with my phone in hand,

and wait for your call to know you'd come home safe.

Some days you'd call late, when it was dark.

Some days it rained, and I'd worry."

Tien looked down at her slippers.

"And yet… I missed the final reward."

Le shook her head softly.

"The coat doesn't make the person, darling.

I don't love you because of your rewards."

She looked toward the horizon,

where the sky met the edge of memory.

And she could almost hear her mother's voice again —

"See that?"

And in that soft pointing

the weight of those years returned –

when love waited without asking,

just so a girl could come home safe.

Chapter 33
The Stitch That Loosens
And the Thread That Never Broke

୬

Tien left home again — this time, not for a competition or school event,

but for university.

There was no scholarship.

Just quiet determination, a frayed bicycle,

and the hope tucked into her mother's salted fish.

The university was big — glossy corridors, city traffic,

students who arrived in private cars or rode scooters that sparkled like chrome birds.

Tien rode her old bicycle.

Her shoes were polished, but her bag was worn.

And she studied.

She studied while others laughed in cafés.

She memorised formulas while they took selfies in air-conditioned lounges.

By the time she graduated, her name was on the list of merit recipients

Academic Excellence, Top 100.

She sent a photo home.

Le framed it in a simple plastic frame and placed it beside a pressed kumquat flower.

"That's my daughter," she told anyone who visited.

"She studied without needing to shout."

After graduation, Tien returned to her province —

not to the village, but to a nearby town where she had been offered a position at the biggest bank.

Le had wrapped the salted fish in wax paper and tied it with red thread
— just enough to keep it closed, not tight.

Beside it, she placed a stack of neatly folded clothes, each stitch small
and sure,

sewn late into nights when the light was too dim and her eyes too tired.

She didn't say much — just adjusted Tien's collar

and patted the edge of her bag,

like she was brushing off dust from a dream.

Tien's bicycle — the same one she rode through muddy paths and
scorching sun — was strapped carefully to the bus's rear compartment.

The frame still held dents from the rainy season,

when she fell twice on the same corner near the rice fields.

The bus rolled forward, and through the glass,

Tien watched her mother grow smaller in the morning light.

No tears. Not yet.

Just the salted weight of home pressed into her lap,

and the quiet hum of the journey ahead.

She didn't know what the city would ask of her —

or how much of herself she'd have to leave behind to belong.

But the bicycle was with her.

And maybe, that was enough.

Later, she saved up and bought a scooter.

It was practical. Easier in the rain. Everyone had one.

Her bicycle — faithful, scratched, and worn —

was sold to a man in the alley behind her boarding house.

He haggled hard.

She let it go for far less than it was worth.

That night, she stared at the empty corner where it used to lean.

A piece of her story had left her hands.

But there was no time for grief — not in the city.

The days came fast.

Meetings. Deadlines. After-hours dinners.

The bank impressed people.

Glass doors. Air conditioning. Perfume that clung to elevator walls.

Tien didn't belong to that world.

But she tried to walk its path —

quiet, diligent, head held just high enough.

One quiet afternoon, she stopped at a street vendor for bánh mì.

The woman behind the cart had worn hands and kind eyes.

As she sliced pickled radish, she asked,

"You look tired, dear. Are you from the countryside?"

Tien blinked. The question caught her off guard.

"Yes. From a small town," she said softly.

"I thought so. You remind me of my daughter — she studied in this city too.

But she changed. The city changes people."

Tien held the warm bánh mì in her hands.

The smell of pâté, coriander, and pork belly stirred something deep.

The woman's voice, the clatter of her knife,

the way she wrapped the bread in paper with care —

it all felt like home.

And suddenly, Tien remembered the red string.

The salted fish.

Her mother's hands smoothing a collar.

The soft thud of a bicycle kickstand on dirt.

Something shifted in her.

She rode back to her boarding house,

holding a warm mug of jasmine tea between her hands

as the sun dropped below the balcony rail.

The smell brought her back —

not to one memory, but to many, layered like fabric:

late nights with her mother,

quiet giggles at the sewing table,

the way jasmine scent always floated through the house,

even when nothing was blooming.

She called Le, as she often did.

At first, nothing unusual.

"I just made tea," Tien said softly.

"Still using the same old mug?" Le asked, a smile in her voice.

They talked about the garden and the weather,

the neighbour's new puppy,

how she'd finally fixed the broken latch on the gate.

She didn't mention Minh. She rarely did anymore.

Tien knew why.

Lan had never liked Minh spending too much time at the old house.

After the wedding, his visits became fewer.

Each one shorter than the last.

Le never complained.

She understood.

Or at least, she tried to.

But Tien could hear it in her mother's pauses —

the way she never quite said I miss him,

only that "the kumquat tree still blooms early every year."

Tien closed her eyes and remembered.

***

It was during her second year at university that Le called with quiet pride:

"I've moved. Just last week."

The old house was gone.

Le had finally saved enough to step into something new.

A real home — bricks, strong doors, no leaking roof.

No more sleeping through storms with a knife beside the bed.

No more bending beneath rain-soaked plastic or broken locks.

"I planted a new kumquat tree in the front garden," she added.

"Not as big as the old one, but it'll bloom.

I wanted something to remind us… of where we started."

Tien helped her unpack that weekend.

She tested every window. Checked every bolt.

She needed to know her mother had shelter now — something solid.

And when she came home for good, years later,

the tree was there — taller now, with a soft scent like memory.

The house felt quiet sometimes.

Minh didn't visit often.

But it no longer creaked beneath the weight of fear.

It held warmth.

And a woman who had earned this peace.

***

Tien took a breath and smiled.

"Mum, I'll come home this weekend," she said.

"Don't do any washing — I'll take care of everything when I get there."

There was a pause.

Then came the soft, familiar sound of Le's chuckle.

Not loud. But full.

"Okay, honey," she said.

"I'll leave the kettle on."

Tien would come home with arms full of laundry.

And a heart still stitched with jasmine scent.

"The kumquat tree blooms early every year."

Le's voice echoed softly in her mind as Tien stood on the balcony, watching the city below — all glass and motion and strangers in suits.

She knew Le hadn't only meant the flowers.

She meant the chairs under the tree.

The jasmine tea.

The quiet dinners with Minh before the world pulled them all in different directions.

That tree had come to mean something more with each passing year
— a place where nothing had to be perfect to feel like home.

279

And as the breeze stirred the curtain beside her,

Tien felt it —

a warmth rising from deep within,

soft but sure.

Maybe going back home was not a step backward.

Maybe it was the right way forward.

Chapter 34
The Kumquat Tree Blooms Again
And the Tree She Planted for Peace

A few months passed. The weekends became more precious than ever — filled with roast duck, small chores, and quiet talks beneath the kumquat tree.

Back in the village, spring had begun again

Saturday morning, the sun rose slow and golden over the village road.

Tien rode her scooter with one hand steady on the roast duck wrapped tight in paper — her mum's favourite.

At the gate, jasmine scent from the kumquat flowers melted into the breeze.

Inside, Le had already set the table — jasmine tea brewed, sweets wrapped in banana leaf.

Tien placed the roast duck down,

changed out of her city clothes,

and reached for the laundry basket – but Le stopped her gently.

"Have tea first. The clothes can wait."

They sat under the old kumquat tree —

two plastic chairs, a chipped table,

the air filled with citrus and jasmine.

Tien took a slow sip.

"Will Minh come tomorrow, Mum?"

Le looked past the leaves.

"I don't know. I never ask."

A pause. Then softly:

"Minh has his own scars.

You weren't born yet."

She stirred the tea gently as she spoke.

"When I married your father, he brought his mother to live with us.

He didn't work.

And… he hated Minh."

Tien blinked.

"He never told me."

Le smiled faintly.

"He wouldn't. He never complains.

It's his strength — and his wound."

She continued, voice steady:

"He was barely ten.

They turned the radio up so he couldn't study.

Your grandma never looked at him with kindness. Just indifference."

Tien listened, quiet.

"One night, I couldn't find him in the house.

Later I found him in your grandma's garden.

He'd tied a hammock between two trees.

He studied there. Slept there. Ate cold rice.

Wouldn't come inside."

Le brushed a fallen kumquat flower from the table.

"Minh survived by staying silent.

That's why now, even with Lan, he avoids conflict.

He's protecting peace the only way he knows how."

Tien looked down at her tea.

The surface trembled with light.

Le smiled gently.

"I understand him.

And I don't blame him.

I just… miss him."

A breeze rustled the leaves above.

A few blossoms dropped, soft against the table.

Tien watched one land beside her cup.

Then she looked at Le, sitting on the chair, gazing toward the horizon.

Her back straightened slightly — still tired from long nights of sewing and the ache that kidney stones had carved into her spine.

This wasn't the garden where Minh once hung his hammock.

That place was long gone.

But here, under the new kumquat tree Le had planted in the front garden, something had taken root.

Not perfect. Not whole. But alive.

Chapter 35
The Coat Doesn't Make the Person
And the Home She Never Left Behind

෪

Sunday morning was still and pale with light.

Tien walked slowly through the streets near her house,

slippers brushing the footpath.

The neighbourhood was waking up —

vendors setting out baskets of herbs,

children laughing in doorways,

the smell of morning broth curling through the air.

She stopped outside a small company

tucked between a bakery and a printing shop.

A simple sign in the window read:

Now hiring: Assistant to the Director.

She looked at it for a long time.

No prestige.

No big salary.

Just… proximity to home.

Tien took a deep breath.

"Okay," she whispered.

"Let it be."

That evening, as the sun dipped low

and the province lights began to flicker,

Le prepared dinner the way she always did before Tien left.

There was some roast duck left from the day before.

She chopped it and braised it with soy sauce, sugar,

and a splash of rice wine.

The kitchen filled with a caramelised, golden smell.

"It's even more beautiful than the original roast duck," Tien joked, lifting the lid.

"Improvised meals always win," Le smiled.

They ate together quietly, the way they always had.

Just shared space, shared breath,

and the warmth of home folded into each bite.

When it was time to leave,

Tien strapped her bag to the scooter,

tightened her helmet.

But just before she turned the key, she looked at her mother.

"Mum," she asked,

"if I'm not a banker in that bank…

will you still be proud of me?"

Le wiped her hands on the dish towel.

Her face unreadable for a moment.

"Of course I am," she said softly.

"I told you — the coat doesn't make the person."

She paused, then asked gently:

"Is everything okay at the bank?"

Tien nodded, her smile light.

"Yes, Mum. My boss said I'm doing well.

I just think… city life is enough for me.

I want something smaller. Something closer."

"Then come back!

I've never doubted you — not since the muffin case."

Tien laughed.

"You still remember that?"

They both laughed.

The kind of laugh that carries memory and trust.

The kind that only happens at the end of something hard,

and the beginning of something true.

"The coat doesn't make the person."

Le's voice echoed gently in Tien's mind as she rode back toward the city.

Along the village road, she passed a little girl carrying a bag too big for her frame — lifting it carefully so it wouldn't scrape the ground.

A memory stirred.

That was once her — barefoot, helping Mum, believing that love was something you did, not just something you felt.

Tien looked back once more, then smiled.

And now, she thought,

Mum's helper should come back home.

Chapter 36
The Tree Still Blooms
And the Peace That Didn't Need Words

෮

Tien came home —

and this time, it was for good.

The small company near her house welcomed her.

She was accepted as the assistant to the director.

The office was small,

but the peace was real.

Minh returned home not long after,

having heard his sister had left her banking job.

He came alone. No mention of Lan.

No need for one.

Perhaps she disapproved.

Perhaps he didn't wait for her permission.

He simply came.

That noon, Le made bánh xèo, just like old times.

When Tien tried to sneak a crispy edge off the pan,

Minh wagged a playful finger:

"Keep the edge thief away from Mum's bánh xèo!"

They laughed until their stomachs hurt.

Tien still stole the edge.

Minh still let her.

The batter sizzled.

The tree bloomed.

And for the first time in a long while,

no one had to say a thing.

Later that evening, when the dishes were done

and the fans stirred warm air through the house,

Le brought out the small plastic table and two old chairs.

Minh pulled another over.

They sat under the kumquat tree again —

just as they used to in the quiet years,

before goodbyes, before distance,

before wounds they never named.

The blossoms were small, white, and fragrant.

They opened toward the sky like nothing had changed.

Le poured jasmine tea.

Minh passed around the cups.

Tien sipped and leaned her shoulder against her mother's.

No stories were told that night.

No pasts explained.

No futures promised.

Only the tree. Only the tea. Only them.

And that was enough.

Chapter 37
The Bench by the Lake
And the Love That Was Let Go

ॐ

A few years had passed since she started her new job in the village,

One afternoon, just before the workday ended, Tien sat by the window, warm tea in hand,

watching the village rooftops glow in the afternoon light.

Somewhere down the road, someone laughed —

young, in love, unburdened.

The sound stirred a memory she hadn't meant to recall.

***

It happened during her season in the village.

He was a friend from her banking years —

a young doctor with steady hands and kind eyes.

They reconnected gently,

with old warmth and new understanding.

Small chats became long conversations.

Then, quietly, something more.

Neither family opposed them.

Not openly.

But both mothers visited fortune tellers —

different shrines, different voices, same result:

"If they marry, one will die young."

That was all it took.

The quiet death of something innocent.

They ended it on a bench near the lake,

under a sky that didn't seem to care.

Tien didn't cry — not then.

She thanked him.

Smiled.

Walked home unbent.

But that night, under her blanket,

the tears came.

Quiet.

Steady.

Unseen.

She told her mother the next day.

Le sat in silence.

Then said, not bitterly but with quiet sorrow:

"I don't know how many innocent couples have been broken up because of a fortune teller."

That was all.

But it told Tien everything.

Le had loved like this, once.

And lost.

This time, though, Tien had chosen differently.

She didn't end it because of fear.

She ended it because she no longer believed fear deserved that power.

It was her first act of letting go —

not in pain,

but in peace.

***

One morning, Tien opened her laptop.

Her heart was quiet —

but not closed.

She didn't believe in fortune tellers anymore.

She believed in something greater.

302

She wasn't chasing love.

But she was no longer afraid to be found by it.

Chapter 38
The Rice That Waited
And the Love That Simmered Slowly

৯৬

She clicked on the dating site.

Not out of desperation —

but because she had stayed long enough.

Now, she would go —

with her mother's blessing in her heart.

One month later, she met someone.

His name was Andrew.

He lived in Australia.

Their first emails were cautious. Polite.

Then one day, he asked:

"Do you believe Jesus is real?"

Tien paused. Then replied:

"Let me Google."

The next day:

"Yes. Jesus is real. Many documents say so.

So… I believe in Him."

They laughed. And kept talking.

Day after day. Night after night.

Their first video call began with a bowl of rice.

Plain. Steaming.

Beside it, a small dish of fish sauce.

Tien smiled at the screen.

Andrew lifted the bowl.

"I used to cook," he said.

"Now I just… eat what's easy.

Restaurants feel lonely."

Tien tilted her head.

"That's all you're having?"

He shrugged.

"It's not bad. Just… quiet."

Tien sent a photo —

her family's mismatched table: salted fish, rice, soup, cucumber.

Not fancy. But full.

"We didn't have much," she wrote.

"But we always had food. And love."

He stared at the photo a long time.

"That's the kind of table I want to come home to."

Chapter 39
The Voice on the Line
And the Love That Spoke Gently

৵

Over the following weeks, their calls became more than habit — they became home.

Their calls became routine.

They laughed. Sang karaoke.

His voice warm. Hers playful.

But it wasn't the singing that deepened things.

It was how he listened.

How he never rushed.

How she never had to explain things twice.

One night, after sharing stories of childhood and faith, he asked:

"Do you believe in God?"

Tien hesitated.

"I want to."

The next day, he sent a Bible app with a reading plan.

"Start with me. We'll go slow."

They read together — Genesis, Psalms, John.

Shared verses.

Talked about truth.

About forgiveness.

About choosing love again and again.

He never pushed.

Never asked her to be more than she was.

And slowly, her heart turned —

not away from her past,

but toward something that could hold it.

One night, she showed him her mum's sewing corner.

Andrew turned his camera to his kitchen —

empty pans, a dishcloth over the sink,

a single rice cooker.

"This place needs someone who knows how to make soup," he said with a smile.

Tien laughed.

"Maybe one day, you won't be holding that bowl alone."

He looked at her —

not just through the screen.

"I think God heard me," he said.

"Even before I knew what to pray for."

The next morning, Tien sat under the kumquat tree with her mother.

Le poured tea, slow and steady.

Tien hesitated.

"There's someone I've been talking to. His name is Andrew."

She paused.

"He lives far. He believes in God. Like me."

Le said nothing at first.

"You'd rather I marry someone nearby," Tien added,

"someone you could meet often."

Le set her cup down gently.

"That first love — the one broken by prophecy…"

it clipped part of your wing."

Tien looked down.

Le reached for her hand.

"This time, you should fly."

312

Tien's eyes filled.

"You're not afraid?"

"I am," Le said.

"But love shouldn't be ruled by fear.

I've lost enough to superstition already."

Then, a faint smile.

"And if he ever dares make fish sauce his dinner again —

tell him I said that's not allowed."

Tien laughed, leaning into her mother's side.

The breeze stirred.

Kumquat blossoms fluttered.

And somewhere, deep inside,

a thread released.

Andrew came to Vietnam.

Sat under the kumquat tree.

Drank jasmine tea with Le.

Tien told him everything — about her father, her dreams, her faith.

She didn't hide anything.

Neither did he.

After hearing it all, Andrew said gently,

"I feel grateful you had such a father who knew how to give to his child.

He didn't give you toys — he gave you science and English books.

That kind of gift shapes the mind early.

It's worth more than a million dollars."

314

And eventually,

they decided to marry.

Chapter 40
After the Rain
And the Peace That Stayed

જી

The wedding was simple, the kind stitched by sincerity rather than spectacle. And not long after, Tien made the hardest decision of her life.

Moving to Australia was the hardest decision of her life —

not because of fear,

but because of Le.

Leaving her mother felt like tearing a thread that had always held.

Only her mother came to the airport.

Tien hadn't told her father — he hadn't spoken to her in years.

But she no longer waited for his voice.

Some absences stop hurting

when the right love remains.

Le, smiling as she tucked salted fish into a box for the flight, said:

"You go now, my dear. You've found someone who speaks truth."

"That's worth crossing oceans for."

Tien hugged her mother tight beneath the kumquat blossoms.

"I'll come home. As often as I can."

"I know you will," Le said.

"But don't rush back just to make me happy.

Live well. That will make me happy."

And so,

after the rain of many years,

a new life began.

Not perfect.

But full of grace.

The first thing Tien did in Australia was plant a kumquat tree.

It wasn't tall — just a slender little thing from the nursery,

its leaves trembling in the wind, unsure if it belonged yet.

Much like her.

She chose a spot in the backyard where the sunlight lingered longest.

The soil was softer than the clay back home,

but dry from days without rain.

She loosened it with her hands anyway,

pressing her fingers into earth that didn't yet feel like home.

As she lowered the sapling into the hole, she whispered,

"Grow well."

Her eyes stayed dry.

Not this time.

But the scent of kumquat leaves — sharp and citrusy —

brought everything back at once:

Her mother's laughter.

The old porch.

The table and chairs for tea beside the tree.

Tien wiped her hands on her pants and stepped back.

It was small. It was fragile.

But it was hers.

***

She stirred slightly.

The memory faded like mist – warm but weightless.

Now, rain whispered against the windows — steady and silver.

She was curled on the couch.

Her husband's hand brushed gently through her hair.

"So you fell asleep, ha?" he said softly.

"Did I?"

"Yes. For a while."

She sat up slowly, pulling the soft blanket around her shoulders.

On the coffee table, her cup of jasmine tea sat untouched and cool.

"I dreamt," she murmured.

"What did you see?"

Her gaze turned toward him, steady now.

"Jesus. Gabriel. And Satan."

He raised an eyebrow — curious but unsurprised.

"Was it dark or light?"

"Light," she said, without hesitation.

"Always light, since I found Him."

They sat in silence.

The kind that doesn't need filling.

From the kitchen came a familiar scent.

Her husband returned with a plate — boiled eggs, halved, salt and pepper on the side.

He set it down with a grin.

"Thought you might be hungry. Look — your legendary salt and pepper boiled egg."

Tien laughed — quiet at first, then full and true.

"Legendary?"

"The best poor girl's feast in the world," he teased.

She laughed again, louder this time.

The sound filled the room like sunlight through clouds.

Their dogs stirred nearby,

lifted their heads to check all was well,

then curled back into their warmth.

Tien leaned into her husband's side.

Outside, the world went on — loud, restless, broken in places.

But inside this home, inside her,

there was something no money could ever buy.

Peace.

And the roots of grace still deepening —

beneath the rain,

beneath the silence,

beneath the tree she planted for hope.

Epilogue
And the Sky That Held Them Both

&

Life in Australia moved quietly, like a river after the storm.

Tien didn't rise through skyscrapers or chase the applause of titles.

But she worked with dignity, kept her heart open,

and found joy in the little things —

tea in the morning, messages from friends,

the way the light touched her kumquat tree by the back fence.

It hadn't bloomed yet, but she didn't mind.

Every morning, she watered it faithfully.

Back in Vietnam, things had changed in small but beautiful ways.

Minh began coming home more often —

not just for the holidays, but for ordinary weekends.

Sometimes he brought groceries.

Sometimes nothing but time.

And with each visit, the silence that had once filled the space between him and Le began to soften.

The old wounds were still there —

but now, there were conversations. Laughter.

Even small arguments about the way to stir the fish sauce.

It was something.

Tien and Le spoke often — daily.

One evening, Tien stepped outside with a cup of jasmine tea

as the sun dipped low.

The call connected, and her mother's voice crackled through the line —

familiar and warm.

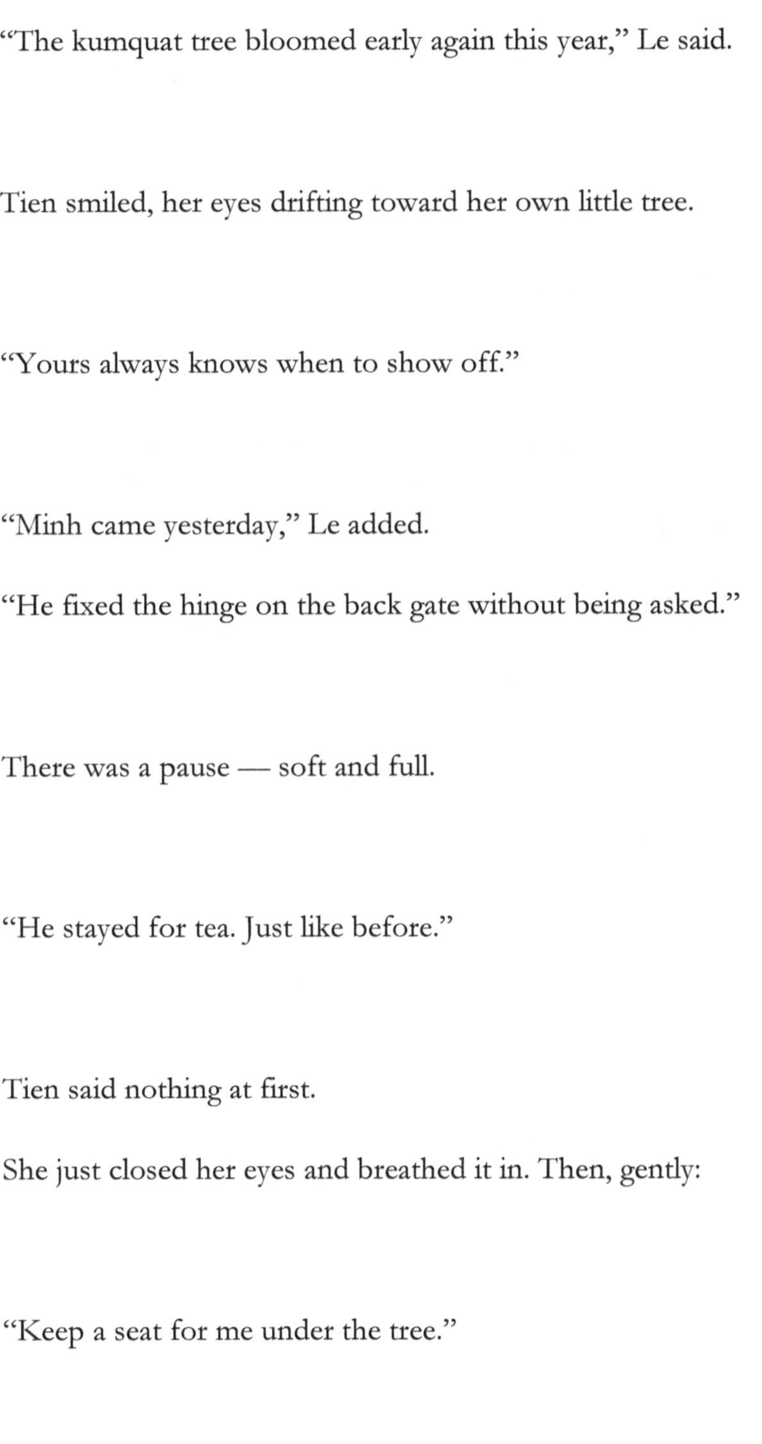

"The kumquat tree bloomed early again this year," Le said.

Tien smiled, her eyes drifting toward her own little tree.

"Yours always knows when to show off."

"Minh came yesterday," Le added.

"He fixed the hinge on the back gate without being asked."

There was a pause — soft and full.

"He stayed for tea. Just like before."

Tien said nothing at first.

She just closed her eyes and breathed it in. Then, gently:

"Keep a seat for me under the tree."

"Always," Le replied.

"It's yours."

Tien smiled, the phone warm in her hand.

Across the ocean, two kumquat trees stood in different soil —

but the same love ran through them both.

This time, it didn't feel like leaving.

It felt like home —

woven from two skies,

rooted in one love.

A Quiet Invitation to Reflect

&

If you've reached the last page, thank you for walking with Tien.

These questions aren't for analysis — but for the heart.

Take what speaks to you. Leave the rest in peace.

1. When words were too heavy, food stepped in.

What dish reminded you of someone you love?

What meal carried a memory in your own life?

2. Silence is everywhere in this story. Not emptiness — but presence.

What kind of love have you received that didn't need words?

And what kind have you given?

3. Le gave without asking anything back.

Which moment between Tien and her mother stayed with you?

What does it mean to be held in quiet strength?

4. Not every injustice in this book was resolved.

And yet, Tien kept walking.

What gave her that strength, do you think?

Have you ever carried hope when no one saw you?

5. Faith came slowly, like a sunrise behind closed eyes.

Did you sense where God stepped in, even before Tien did?

Have there been quiet moments in your own life where grace felt close?

6. Minh came home — not loudly, but lovingly.

Have you ever been surprised by someone showing up, even when they didn't have to?

What kind of protection or connection lives quietly in your own life?

7. The ending wasn't grand. It was peace.

After the rain, Tien didn't rise to fame — she found stillness.

What does "healing" mean to you now?

Where are you in your own story?

Your Turn

What would you tell the younger version of yourself — or
vice versa — if she were sitting beside you now?

Dishes Woven Through the Journey

These are the meals that lived alongside the memories.

Some were cooked in joy, others in silence.

Some came from celebration, some from survival.

But each one — whether congee, salted fish, or sweet tonic — was a

quiet offering of love.

I share them here not just as recipes,

but as threads of a life:

stitched in rice, salted with sacrifice, and carried across oceans.

From our table to yours —

may these dishes nourish your body, and your heart.

Broken Rice with Grilled Pork Skin (Cơm Tấm Bì)	29	41
Stir-Fried Green Beans with Thin Pork Slices	32	45
Braised Roast Duck with Soy Sauce	35	47

Boiled Egg with Salt & Pepper

From Chapter 1 – The Day the Rain Came

A daily gift from Le to baby Tien. One egg, never shared, always given.

Ingredients

- 1 egg
- Pinch of salt
- Crack of black pepper
- (Optional: squeeze of lime will enhance the flavour)

Boiling Time Guide

Bring a pot of water to a gentle boil, then lower in the egg carefully. Cook according to your preference:

- Soft (runny yolk): 6 minutes
- Medium (jammy centre): 8 minutes
- Well-done (firm yolk): 10–11 minutes

After boiling, transfer the egg immediately to a bowl of cold water for 1–2 minutes. This stops the cooking and makes peeling easier.

To Serve

Peel gently. Slice in half or leave whole.

Sprinkle with salt and pepper.

If desired, serve with rice and cucumber slices for a complete village-style meal.

Memory Note

Le raised a chicken so there would be one egg each day.

Even when the house had no food, the egg always went to Tien.

It was her mother's unspoken prayer:

"You first, darling Always you first."

Fried Egg with Rice and Boiled Greens

From Chapter 5 – The Strongest Silence

A simple meal, offered without questions. A bowl that said: "You don't have to carry this alone."

Ingredients

- 1 egg
- 1 bowl of steamed jasmine rice
- A handful of Asian greens (bok choy, mustard greens, or spinach)
- Pinch of salt
- A dash of soy sauce or fish sauce with red chilli (optional)
- 1–2 tsp cooking oil

Instructions

1. Steam the rice and keep warm.

2. Boil the greens in lightly salted water for 1–2 minutes until just tender. Drain and set aside.

3. In a small non-stick or well-seasoned pan, heat the oil on high until shimmering.

4. Crack in the egg without swirling — let it sit.

5. Cook without moving until the white puffs and edges go golden and lacy.

For a runny yolk: 2–3 minutes.

For firmer: flip and cook another 1–2 minutes.

Crispy Edge Tip

To get that signature golden, crackly edge, make sure your oil is hot enough before the egg goes in. You should hear a gentle sizzle. Don't stir or flip too soon — just let it crisp.

To Serve

Place rice in a bowl. Top with the fried egg and arrange the greens beside it. Add a drizzle of soy or fish sauce if desired.

Eat warm. Eat slow.

Memory Note

Le didn't need the story.

She just pushed the egg closer.

Sometimes healing begins with a bowl — and the quiet permission to feel safe.

Shallot Omelette

From Chapter 7 – Mila

A quiet breakfast. Tears masked by shallots. A mother who never wanted her daughter to see her cry.

Ingredients

- 2 eggs
- 1 small shallot, finely sliced
- 1 tsp fish sauce
- Oil for frying

Instructions

1. In a bowl, beat the eggs with the sliced shallot and fish sauce.
2. Heat a small pan over medium heat and add a little oil.
3. When the oil is hot, pour in the egg mixture.
4. Let it cook undisturbed until the bottom is golden, then gently flip to cook the other side.
5. Cook until set, with slightly crisp edges and soft inside.

To Serve

Slide onto a plate. Serve with hot rice.

Eat while it's warm, or quietly cold.

Sometimes, love looks like this.

Memory Note

"There's no onion in the omelette," Tien said.

Le wiped her cheek.

"Must've been a long sewing night."

Minced Pork Congee

From Chapter 7 – Mila

The bowl that waited without judgment. A quiet knowing. A meal for grief and soft goodbyes.

Ingredients

- ½ cup jasmine rice, rinsed
- 2 L water or pork broth
- 150 g minced pork
- 4 cloves garlic, minced
- ½ small onion, finely diced
- 1 tbsp fish sauce
- ½ tsp white pepper
- 1 tsp salt
- Pinch of sugar
- Pinch of MSG (optional)
- Spring onion or coriander, chopped (for garnish)

Instructions

1. In a medium pot over medium-high heat, add a little oil. When hot, stir in the garlic.

2. Once the garlic turns golden, quickly add the minced pork and stir for about 30 seconds.

3. Add the rinsed rice and broth. Bring to a boil, then reduce to a gentle simmer.

4. Stir occasionally, gently breaking the rice with the back of a spoon as it softens. Simmer for 30–40 minutes, until the congee becomes thick and creamy.

5.   Season with fish sauce, pepper, salt, MSG (if using), and a pinch of sugar.

6.   Stir in the cooked pork mixture.

7.   Taste and adjust seasoning. Keep warm until ready to serve.

To Serve

Ladle into bowls. Garnish with fresh herbs, or add a soft-boiled egg if desired.

Eat with a quiet spoon.

Memory Note

She made extra.
Not because she was asked —
but because she saw.

This was more than food.
It was recognition —
of what had been carried,
and what had been lost.

Roasted Peanuts with Salt and Lime Leaves

From Chapter 8 – Home, When He's Here

A bowl brought out without occasion. A soft offering in a loud world.

Ingredients

- 1 cup raw peanuts (skin on or off)
- 3–4 kaffir lime leaves (fresh or dried), sliced very thin
- ½ tsp salt
- 1 tsp oil (optional, for added fragrance)

Instructions

1. In a dry pan over medium heat, roast the peanuts gently, stirring often to avoid burning.
Toast for 8–10 minutes until golden and fragrant.
2. In the last 1–2 minutes, add the sliced lime leaves and continue stirring until crisp and aromatic.
3. Turn off the heat. While still warm, sprinkle in the salt and toss everything together.
If desired, add a small spoon of oil before serving for extra aroma.

To Serve

Let cool slightly. Serve in a shallow bowl with tea or over quiet conversation.

Store in an airtight jar for a few days of comfort.

Memory Note

The crunch echoed softly under the hum of the old TV.

No occasion. No audience.

Just the taste of being thought of.

Sweet & Sour Fish Soup (Canh Chua Cá)

From Chapter 9 – The Bitterness of Sweet & Sour

A bowl made with sacrifice. Her favourite, offered in a time of lack —
not because she asked, but because she was loved.

Ingredients

- 500 g firm white fish (such as basa, snapper, or perch), cleaned and cut into 3–4 pieces
- ¼ pineapple, cut into small wedges
- 1 medium tomato, cut into wedges
- A few pieces of okra, taro stem (elephant ear), or morning glory (optional, or to taste)
- A handful of Thai basil or sawtooth herb, chopped
- 1 tbsp tamarind paste (adjust to taste)
- 1 tbsp fish sauce
- 2 tsp sugar
- 1 L water
- 1 tsp minced garlic
- Salt and MSG to taste
- Cooking oil

Instructions

1. In a pot, heat a little oil and sauté the garlic until golden.
2. Add water and tamarind paste. Stir to dissolve. Bring to a gentle simmer and add half the chopped herbs.
3. Stir in sugar, fish sauce, salt, and MSG. Add the fish pieces and simmer for about 10 minutes, then gently remove the fish and set aside.

4. Add pineapple and okra or taro stem (if using). Simmer for 5–10 minutes.

5. Add remaining vegetables and cook for another 3–5 minutes, then return the fish to the pot to warm through.

6. Just before serving, add the rest of the herbs for fragrance.

To Serve

Place a piece of fish into each bowl. Ladle the fragrant broth and vegetables over the top.

Serve with steamed rice — and silence, if needed.

Memory Note

The fish was placed in her bowl —
without fuss,
without drama.

And in that small act,
she tasted the fullness
of her mother's heart.

Banana Muffins

From Chapter 10 – Muffins and Misunderstandings

A box of sweet banana muffins. Bought with effort. Misread in silence. Remembered forever.

Ingredients

(Makes 6 small muffins)

- 2 ripe bananas, mashed
- 1 egg
- ¼ cup sugar
- ¼ cup milk
- ¼ cup neutral oil or melted butter
- 1 cup self-raising flour
- Pinch of salt
- ½ tsp vanilla (optional)

Instructions

1. Preheat oven to 170°C (340°F). Line a muffin tray with 6 paper cups.
2. In a medium bowl, mix mashed bananas with egg, sugar, milk, and oil until combined.
3. Fold in the flour, salt, and vanilla (if using) until just mixed — do not over stir.
4. Spoon the batter evenly into the cups, filling each about ¾ full.
5. Bake for 18–22 minutes, until lightly golden and risen.

Let cool in the tray for 5 minutes, then transfer to a wire rack.

To Serve

Place in a small container or bag.
It doesn't need to be fancy.
Only full of love.

Memory Note

She didn't cry
when her mum didn't open it.

Because even unopened,
the muffin carried
everything she wanted to say.

Fish Congee with Ginger and Shallot

From Chapter 11 – The Stitch That Hold

A bowl made after the music stopped. A daughter's quiet act of love — for the mother who always fed her first.

Ingredients

- ½ cup jasmine rice, rinsed well
- 1.5 L water or light chicken broth
- 150 g white fish fillet (basa, snapper, or perch), boneless
- 5–6 slices fresh ginger
- 1 shallot, thinly sliced
- A few coriander leaves, thinly sliced
- ½ tsp salt
- Pinch of sugar
- MSG (optional)
- White pepper to taste
- Optional: fried shallots or a dash of sesame oil

Instructions

1. In a medium pot, bring the water or broth to a boil. Add the fish and ginger slices. Let the fish poach gently for 5–7 minutes until just cooked through.
2. Remove the fish and ginger, place on a plate, and set aside.
3. In a separate pot, combine the rinsed rice and remaining liquid. Bring to a boil, then reduce to a simmer.
4. Stir occasionally, allowing the rice to break down and thicken — about 30–40 minutes.

5.   Season with salt, sugar, MSG (if using), and a pinch of white pepper.

6.   Gently flake the fish into the congee and simmer for another 5 minutes.

To Serve

Ladle into a deep bowl.

Top with sliced shallot and coriander — add fried shallots or sesame oil if you wish.

Hold it in your hands like a soft healing.

Memory Note

She didn't speak
when she gave it to her mum.
The scent did all the talking.
It said:
"You don't have to be strong tonight. I'm here."

Braised Fish with Caramel Sauce (Cá Kho Tộ)

From Chapter 12 – The Braised Fish

A dish that taught more than any lecture. A bite that carried history, sacrifice, and the silence of a boy who brought dinner home from the river.

Ingredients

- 300 g firm fish (catfish, basa, or mackerel), cut into thick pieces
- 2 tbsp sugar
- 2 tbsp fish sauce
- 2 garlic cloves, minced
- 2 shallots, thinly sliced
- A few slices of chilli (optional)
- ½ tsp cracked black pepper
- ½ cup coconut water (or plain water)
- 1 tbsp oil

Instructions

1. In a clay or heavy-bottomed pan, melt 1 tablespoon of sugar over medium-low heat until it turns a deep golden caramel. Watch carefully to avoid burning.

2. Add oil and minced garlic. Stir briefly until fragrant.

3. Add the fish pieces and sear both sides in the caramel base.

4. Pour in fish sauce, remaining sugar, chilli, pepper, and coconut water.

5.	Bring to a gentle simmer, then reduce heat to low. Cover and braise for 20–30 minutes, flipping the fish once halfway through.

6.	Uncover for the final 5 minutes, letting the sauce reduce to a sticky, glossy glaze.

7.	Just before serving, scatter the sliced shallots over the top.

To Serve

Spoon over steaming white rice.
Or, if there's only one piece left — wrap it gently,
and remember where it came from.

Memory Note

She almost threw it away.

But then she heard the story of her brother…
and the coconut shell
that helped feed them all.

Vietnamese Duck Curry with Taro (Cà Ri Vịt)

From Chapter 13 – The Sweet Fruit

A dish of joy and quiet triumph. Cooked when Tien rose to the top —
not with pride, but with quiet awe.

Ingredients

- ½ duck (about 1 kg), cleaned and chopped into serving pieces
- 400 g taro, peeled and cut into large cubes (1.5–2 cm)
- 2 tbsp Vietnamese or Malaysian-style curry powder
- 1 tbsp cooking wine (optional)
- 1 tbsp fish sauce
- 2 tbsp sugar
- 1 tsp salt
- 3 garlic cloves, minced
- 1 onion, sliced
- 400 ml coconut milk
- 500 ml water or chicken broth
- 1 tbsp oil
- 1 lemongrass stalk, bruised
- 1 large slice of chilli

Instructions

1. Marinate the duck with curry powder, fish sauce, sugar, cooking wine (if using), garlic, salt, and a touch of pepper. Let sit for at least 1 hour.
2. In a large pot, heat oil and sauté the lemongrass and chilli with minced onion until soft and fragrant.

3.	Add the marinated duck pieces and sear until the skin begins to brown slightly.

4.	Pour in coconut milk and water. Stir gently, cover, and simmer for 30–40 minutes until the duck is tender.

5.	Meanwhile, in a separate pan, deep-fry the taro cubes until lightly golden — this helps them stay intact in the curry.

6.	Add the taro to the pot and simmer for another 5 minutes, until the curry is thick, rich, and fragrant.

To Serve

Ladle into deep bowls.

Enjoy with vermicelli noodles, crusty Vietnamese bread, or simple white rice —

and the kind of laughter that doesn't need words.

Memory Note

She didn't need trophies.
The duck curry was her reward.

A meal made slowly, with love.
A bowl that said,
"You made it, my darling. And I saw it all."

Pan-Fried Lemongrass Pork Chops

From Chapter 15 – The Quiet Flame

The first dish she learned beside her mother. A recipe that filled the air with love before it ever touched the plate.

Ingredients

- 2 pork loin chops, bone-in or boneless
- 1 stalk lemongrass, white part only, finely minced
- 2 garlic cloves, crushed
- 1 tbsp soy sauce
- 1 tsp sugar
- Black pepper to taste
- 1–2 tsp oil for frying

Instructions

1. Tenderise pork chops slightly with a mallet or the back of a knife.
2. Marinate with lemongrass, garlic, soy sauce, sugar, and pepper. Let sit 30 minutes or overnight.
3. Heat oil in a pan over medium heat.
4. Add pork chops and sear 3–4 minutes each side, or until golden, with caramelised edges and cooked through.
5. Let rest a minute before serving.

To Serve

With rice.

Cucumber slices.

Add soy sauce and chilli for dipping if desire

And a mother's quiet story shared between bites.

Memory Note

The heat carried the scent like music.
And from the very first time she held the pan,
Tien didn't just learn to cook —
She learned to care the same way her mother did.

Clear Pork Soup with Carrot and Radish

From Chapter 16 – The Price of Light

A pot simmered for hope. Made with quiet urgency when eyesight faded, and comfort was all that could be offered.

Ingredients

- 300 g pork ribs or pork bones, chopped into 3–4 cm pieces
- 1 large carrot, peeled and sliced into 2 cm rounds
- 1 small white radish, peeled and sliced into 2 cm rounds
- 1.2 L water
- 1 tsp salt
- 1 tsp sugar
- Pinch of MSG (optional)
- 1 tbsp fish sauce
- 1 tbsp oil
- Minced garlic (1 clove)
- Chopped shallot or coriander (for garnish)

Instructions

1. Blanch the pork ribs in boiling water for a minute to remove impurities. Rinse and drain.

2. In a clean pot over medium heat, add oil and sauté the minced garlic until golden.

3. Add the pork ribs and pour in 1.2 litres of water. Bring to a boil, then reduce to a gentle simmer.

4.   Season with salt, sugar, and MSG (if using). Skim off any foam. Simmer for 30 minutes.

5.   Add the carrot and radish. Continue simmering for another 20–30 minutes, until the vegetables are tender and the broth is aromatic.

6.   Stir in the fish sauce and cook for another 2 minutes.

To Serve

Ladle into deep bowls.

Serve with rice — and a quiet moment.

No words needed — just the scent of someone who still believes you can heal.

Memory Note

"Carrot is good for your eyes," she said, as the soup bubbled.

It wasn't science.

It was faith.

In a kitchen. In a girl.

In the kind of love

that never stops trying.

Mung Bean Congee with Coconut Milk
(Chè Đậu Xanh)

From Chapter 19 – The Shield

A warm bowl served like a hug. For eyes that ached. For hearts that needed quiet holding.

Ingredients

- ½ cup split mung beans (hulled)
- 1l water
- 250gr sugar (adjust to taste)
- 200ml coconut milk
- 1–2 pandan leaves, tied in a knot (or ½ tsp pandan essence) (optional)
- Pinch of salt

Instructions

1.   Rinse mung beans well.

Optional: Soak for 30 minutes to shorten cooking time.

2.   In a pot, combine mung beans, water, and pandan leaves.

Bring to a boil, then reduce to a gentle simmer.

Cook for 20–30 minutes until beans are soft and broken down.

3.   Add sugar and a pinch of salt. Stir to dissolve.

4.   Pour in coconut milk. Simmer another 5 minutes until creamy and fragrant.

Remove pandan leaves.

To Serve

Serve warm, in small bowls.

Eat slowly. Let the sweetness settle in places that medicine cannot reach.

Memory Note

"Good for your eyes," she said.

But it wasn't just for vision.

It was for the moments her daughter needed to be seen.

Crispy Fried Fish with Ginger Sauce

From Chapter 20 – The Singer of the House

A crackling dish made for the ones she loved. It wasn't the music that brought them together — it was the smell of fish and the care in her hands.

Ingredients

For the fish:

- 2 small whole fish (mackerel, tilapia, or river fish), cleaned and patted dry
- Salt and pepper
- Plain flour, for coating
- Oil, for frying

For the sauce:

- 1 tbsp fish sauce
- 1 tbsp sugar
- 1 tbsp lemon or lime juice
- 1 small knob of ginger, julienned
- 1 fresh red chilli, sliced (optional)
- 2 tbsp water

Instructions

1. Prepare the fish: Lightly season both sides with salt and pepper. Let rest for 10 minutes. Lightly coat with flour and shake off any excess.
2. Heat oil in a pan over medium heat. Fry the fish until golden and crispy on both sides — about 5–6 minutes per

side, depending on thickness. Remove and drain on paper towel.

3.   In a small saucepan, combine all sauce ingredients. Warm gently over low heat until fragrant and slightly thickened — just a minute or two.

4.   Spoon the sauce over the fried fish just before serving.

To Serve

Serve with jasmine rice, cucumber, and quiet conversation.
A dish made with care — not noise.

Memory Note

Tien came running, dragging Mai with her.
"I smelled the ginger from the hallway!"

Le didn't say much.

She just cooked
with the kind of love
that doesn't need permission
to be beautiful.

Sweet & Sour Salted Fish with White Rice

From Chapter 21 – The Taste of Memory

A dish cooked with memory. Sharp, sweet, honest. A reminder that even the simplest meals can carry generations.

Ingredients

- 1 piece of salted fish (cá khô), about 80–100g
- 2.5 tbsp sugar
- 2.5 tbsp vinegar (rice or white)
- 1 garlic clove, minced
- 1 red chilli, sliced
- 1 tbsp water
- 1 tsp oil

To accompany:

- Steamed jasmine rice
- Fresh cucumber, sliced thin

Instructions

1. Soak salted fish in lukewarm water for 20–30 minutes to reduce saltiness. Pat dry.

2. Heat oil in a pan and pan-fry the fish until golden and crisp on both sides.

3. In a small bowl, mix sugar, vinegar, water, garlic, and chilli.

4. Remove fish and set aside.

Pour sauce into the same pan, stir and let it bubble until slightly thickened (about 1 minute).

5.   Return the fish to the pan and coat in sauce briefly.

To Serve

Place over white rice.

Add cucumber slices.

Eat slow, like you're remembering something important.

Memory Note

It wasn't a feast. Just rice and salted fish.

But to Tien, it tasted like the kind of love that survives hard years —
and still shines.

Bánh Xèo (Vietnamese Crispy Sizzling Crepes)

From Chapter 24 – The Edge of Bánh Xèo

A crackling crepe. A playful finger. And the taste of something whole again, shared in laughter.

Ingredients

(Makes about 6 small crepes)

For the batter:

- ½ cup rice flour
- ½ cup corn starch
- ¼ cup plain flour (optional, for extra crispness)
- 1 tsp turmeric powder
- 400 ml lukewarm water
- 150 ml coconut milk (optional, for extra richness)
- ½ tsp salt
- 1 tsp sugar
- 1 egg
- 2 spring onions, thinly sliced

For the filling:

- 100 g pork belly or shoulder, thinly sliced
- 100 g shrimp, peeled and deveined
- ½ cup boiled mung beans (optional)
- A large handful of bean sprouts
- Salt and pepper, to taste
- Oil for frying

To serve:

- Fresh herbs: mint, lettuce, perilla, coriander, mustard cabbage
- Vietnamese sweet & sour fish sauce (nước mắm chua ngọt)
- Rice paper or extra lettuce for wrapping (optional)

Instructions

1. Make the batter: In a bowl, whisk together rice flour, corn starch, turmeric, salt, sugar, coconut milk, lukewarm water, and egg until smooth. Stir in the spring onions. Let the batter rest for 1–2 hours.

2. Prepare the filling: Wash the bean sprouts and let them dry. Season the pork and shrimp lightly with salt and pepper.

3. In a small non-stick pan, heat 1 tsp of oil over medium-high heat. Sauté the pork and shrimp briefly until just cooked.

4. Pour a thin layer of batter into the pan, swirling to spread evenly.

5. Scatter bean sprouts and mung beans over the top. Cover the pan and cook for 2–3 minutes.

6. Uncover and continue cooking until the edges are crisp and golden.

7. Fold the crepe in half and slide onto a serving plate.

To Serve

Wrap pieces of the crepe in fresh herbs or lettuce.

Dip in sweet & sour fish sauce.

Eat quickly — the crisp edge is for the quick and bold.

Memory Note

The edge thief struck again. Minh laughed.

Le didn't scold.

That crackling crepe said what no one dared to:

We're still a family. We're still here.

34

Jujube-Lotus Tonic with Longan

From Chapter 25 – The Golden Sip

A sweet, simmered promise. Not for celebration, but for comfort. A bowl that said: "You don't have to earn love. You already have it."

Ingredients

- 10 dried red jujubes (red dates)
- 1/3 cup lotus seeds (dried or fresh, green core removed)
- ½ cup dried longan
- 1 tbsp rock sugar (or to taste)
- 4 cups water

Instructions

1. Rinse all ingredients well. If using dried lotus seeds, soak for 1–2 hours beforehand.

2. In a pot, add water, lotus seeds, and jujubes. Bring to a gentle boil, then simmer for 30–40 minutes until soft.

3. Add longan and rock sugar. Simmer another 5–10 minutes until fragrant and slightly syrupy.

4. Remove ginger slices before serving, or leave for warmth.

To Serve

Serve warm, in a small bowl.

Best taken quietly, when you're tired of chasing things.

Memory Note

She didn't say, "Well done."
She just said, "Drink this."
And in that golden broth, Tien tasted something better than praise —
unconditional love.

Chicken Congee (Cháo Gà)

From Chapter 26 – The Province Seat

A bowl made for celebration, not recovery. Light, warm, and filled with quiet pride — because Tien had risen, and her mother had known all along she could.

Ingredients

- ½ cup jasmine rice, rinsed
- 1 chicken thigh or small chicken breast (bone-in for deeper flavour)
- 1.2 L water
- 1 onion, peeled
- 1 tsp salt
- Pinch of MSG (optional)
- 1 tsp sugar
- 1 tbsp fish sauce
- Spring onion and coriander, for garnish
- Fried shallots (optional)
- 1 garlic clove, minced
- 1 tbsp oil

Instructions

1. In a pot over medium heat, add oil and sauté the minced garlic until golden.
2. Add the chicken, water, onion, salt, sugar, and MSG. Simmer gently for 30 minutes.
3. Remove the chicken, slice thinly, and set aside.

4.   Add the rinsed rice to the broth. Simmer for 30–40 minutes, stirring occasionally, until soft and creamy.

5.   Stir in the fish sauce. Let simmer a few more minutes to bring the flavours together.

To Serve

Spoon into bowls. Top with coriander, spring onion, and fried shallots if desired.

Eat slowly — like something has just gone right.

Memory Note

They didn't make a fuss about her results.

They just ladled congee into a bowl —

and let her know

she was seen.

Banana Tree Salad (Gỏi Bắp Chuối)

Also from Chapter 26 – The Province Seat

Fresh, sharp, a little wild. A victory salad made not for ceremony, but for a girl who surprised them all — quietly, completely.

Ingredients

- 1 small banana tree, outer layers removed
- Juice of 1 lime or 1 tbsp vinegar (for soaking)
- 100 g poached chicken or pork (optional), shredded
- 1 small carrot, julienned (optional)
- Vietnamese herbs: mint, coriander, perilla
- Crushed roasted peanuts
- Fried shallots (optional)

For the dressing (nước mắm base):

- 1 tbsp fish sauce
- 1 tbsp lime or lemon juice
- 1 tbsp sugar
- 1 garlic clove, minced
- 1 small red chilli, sliced
- 2 tbsp water

Instructions

1. Slice the banana tree thinly and soak in lime water for 15–20 minutes to prevent browning. Rinse and drain.
2. Mix dressing ingredients until the sugar fully dissolves.

3.	Toss the banana tree with herbs, shredded meat (if using), carrot (if using), and dressing.

4.	Top with peanuts and fried shallots.

To Serve

Serve chilled or at room temperature. Pile it high.
Crunch. Sip. Breathe in the scent of lime and crushed leaves.

Memory Note

It wasn't a rich meal.

But with banana tree,
chicken congee,
and music under her fingers —

Tien felt full.
In every sense.

Broken Rice with Grilled Pork Skin (Cơm Tấm Bì)

From Chapter 29 – The Broken Rice Year

A dish eaten in silence. A restaurant that didn't ask questions. And a plate that held more kindness than home sometimes could.

Ingredients

For the rice:

- 1 cup broken rice (gạo tấm), rinsed
- Water, for cooking

For the shredded pork skin (bì):

- 200 g pork skin, boiled and sliced very thinly (or use pre-shredded pork skin from a Vietnamese store)
- 1 tbsp roasted rice powder (thính gạo)
- Pinch of salt and sugar

For the grilled pork (optional):

- 200 g pork shoulder or pork chop
- Marinade: lemongrass, garlic, soy sauce, sugar, and pepper
- Grill or pan-fry until golden and slightly charred

For the dipping sauce (nước mắm chua ngọt):

- 1 tbsp fish sauce
- 1 tbsp sugar
- 1 tbsp lime juice

* 1–2 tbsp water
* 1 garlic clove, minced
* 1 small red chilli, sliced

Optional:

* 1 egg, fried sunny-side up
* Cucumber, tomato slices, or pickled carrots for serving

Instructions

1. Cook broken rice like jasmine rice, using slightly less water for a firmer texture.

2. Mix the thinly sliced pork skin with roasted rice powder, a pinch of salt, and sugar. Set aside.

3. If using grilled pork, marinate for at least 30 minutes, then grill or pan-fry until golden and caramelised.

4. Mix all dipping sauce ingredients in a small bowl until the sugar fully dissolves.

To Serve

Scoop warm broken rice onto a plate.

Top with shredded pork skin, grilled pork, and a fried egg if desired.

Spoon the sauce over the top.

Serve with cucumber slices, tomato, or pickled carrot.

Memory Note

No one asked her to smile.

No one whispered behind her back.

The rice was cracked.
The pork skin humble.

But Tien left that table
feeling whole.

Stir-Fried Green Beans with Thin Pork Slices

From Chapter 32 – The Name That Disappeared

A quiet dinner. No congratulations. No questions. Just a warm plate and a mother who said: "Come eat, honey."

Ingredients

- 100 g pork loin, belly, or shoulder, thinly sliced
- 200 g green beans, trimmed
- 2 garlic cloves, minced
- ½ tsp sugar
- 1 tsp oyster sauce (optional)
- A dash of water
- Salt and pepper, to taste
- 1 tsp oil

Instructions

1. Blanch the green beans in boiling water for 1–2 minutes. Drain and set aside.

2. Heat oil in a pan over medium heat. Add garlic and pork slices. Stir-fry until the pork begins to brown.

3. Add the green beans, sugar, oyster sauce (if using), and a splash of water.

4. Stir-fry for 2–3 more minutes until the beans are crisp-tender and coated in flavour.

5. Season to taste with salt and pepper.

To Serve

Serve with hot steamed rice and a small dish of soy sauce with sliced red chilli.

Eat in silence.

Let it speak louder than applause.

Memory Note

She didn't say anything
about the ceremony.

But she gave her daughter
the meat,
the spice,
the warmth —

and a place
where she was still worthy.

Braised Roast Duck with Soy Sauce

From Chapter 35 – The Coat Doesn't Make the Person

A dish made not to impress, but to remember. A quiet meal before a goodbye, filled with the warmth of yesterday's roast and the tenderness of a mother's hands.

Ingredients

- 200–300g roast duck (leftover or store-bought), chopped into bite-sized pieces
- 1 tbsp soy sauce
- 1 tsp dark soy sauce (optional, for colour)
- 1 tsp sugar
- 1 tbsp rice wine or Shaoxing wine
- 1 garlic clove, minced
- 100ml of water
- Spring onion or coriander, chopped (optional, to garnish)

Instructions

1. Heat a small pan over medium heat. Add a dash of oil.
2. Sauté the minced garlic until fragrant, about 30 seconds.
3. Add the chopped roast duck and stir gently.
4. Pour in soy sauce, dark soy sauce (if using), sugar, and rice wine. Stir to coat the duck evenly.
5. Add water.
6. Simmer for 5–7 minutes.

7.   Taste and adjust seasoning if needed. Some ducks are already salty, so balance gently.

8.   Garnish with spring onion or coriander, if desired.

48

To Serve

Spoon over warm white rice.

Eat quietly, letting the soy-rich scent carry memory to the table.

Memory Note

It wasn't fancy.

But it tasted like the days before leaving —

when everything ordinary felt like something worth holding onto.

Acknowledgements

ϧ

I thank God first — my Father, my Shepherd, and my quiet strength.

Through every silence, storm, and beginning, He has carried me.

This story belongs to Him before it belongs to me.

To my husband, Andrew — thank you for being part of this journey.

Our story continues to shape me, and I carry it with grace.

To my mother — Mẹ — every chapter carries your hands, your strength, your love.

You never asked to be praised, but your sacrifices shaped who I am.

You are the thread that never broke.

To my brother, Minh — thank you for being my quiet shield.

You never said much, but you always gave more than words.

Even the edges of bánh xèo.

To Pastor Paul — Thank you for being the shepherd who gently led us toward the truth. You didn't just speak of God's love — you lived it.

Your quiet generosity, steady faith, and open heart were the beginning of a new chapter in our lives. You brought my husband and me to Christ, and through that, everything changed.

This book would not exist without the grace that first found us through you.

To my church brothers and sisters, who supported me through the hardest season in Australia — your kindness, prayers, and care gave me more strength than you know.

And to every friend, teacher, neighbour, reader, and soul who crossed my path —

thank you.

Whether you stayed for a season or a moment, your presence left something behind.

A word. A kindness. A spark of light.

You helped me grow, gently, toward who I am today.

And I carry your thread in this tapestry too.

From the quiet corners of my heart —

thank you for being part of my journey.

The words shared by readers in this book were offered with kindness
and permission.

Each one is a thread of encouragement — gently woven into the pages
by hearts who walked with me.

I carry their trust with gratitude.

About the Author

Angel Tien Le was born in Vietnam and now lives in Australia. She finds joy in writing, baking, cooking, and quiet moments with God. Her journey — woven with hardship, resilience, and grace — inspires the stories she shares.

Woven by Love is her first book: a tapestry of memory, faith, and quiet healing. Through Tien's voice, Angel honours the strength of women who carry invisible burdens and choose love again and again.

In her free time, Angel enjoys tending her garden, playing the piano, taking care of her two dogs, and crafting Vietnamese dishes that connect generations.

She hopes her words bring comfort to those walking in silence — and remind them that healing is possible, even in the quietest places.

To connect with Angel or share your thoughts on Woven by Love, you can reach her at:

Website: www.AngelTienLe.com

Email: angelwrites2212@gmail.com

restraint. It left me wondering — not only as her husband, but as a reader — how many hearts this book will touch."

Andrew Le
MBBS (UNSW),
Author's beloved husband.

"Angel writes so beautifully and I was hooked from the moment I read the first page. I tried not to read too fast, as every page was so moving and touched my heart. Her faith, strength and determination are an encouragement to us all."

Jackie S.
PhD in Optometry.

"*Woven by Love* is a beautifully crafted story that follows the emotional and inspiring journey of Tien, a young girl growing up in poverty and hardship. It's both moving and uplifting, reminding us of the power of perseverance and hope. As a delightful bonus, there are recipes included at the end of the book!"

Jean Leung

"A beautiful account of Angel's life struggling through hardship but also wonderfully touching moments with those who helped make her the strong and caring person that she is today. A great reminder of how great our God is and how he works in unexpected ways to shape our lives. A beautiful read and insight into this wonderful author."

Jennifer T.

What Readers Say

&

"*Woven by Love* is more than a memoir — it's a testimony of faith, grace, and the quiet power of a mother's love. Angel writes with gentleness and spiritual clarity. Her story will speak deeply to hearts that have endured much."

Paul Tai Huynh
Pastor, PhD in Christian Counseling.

"It (*Woven by Love*) made me laugh.
It made me cry.
It made me remember things from my childhood that had dimmed in my memory.
It made me remember things that made me stronger and the things that brought me pain, that God helped me to overcome with forgiveness."

Judy Bell

"When I read the chapter 'The Strongest Silence,' my heart skipped a beat — no, actually quite a few beats. Angel captured the world through the eyes of a five-year-old girl facing cruelty from her friends — not with bitterness, but with a tender strength that is truly remarkable. The way little Tien hides her wounds to protect her mother reveals a love so quiet, yet so powerful. Writing from a child's point of view is incredibly difficult, but Angel did it with rare beauty and

Coming Soon

The story does not end here.

There are still threads left unwoven—
carried across distance,
through silence,
and into a life that is still learning how to hold love.

In *Woven by Love: The Second Thread*, the journey continues.

Tien comes to Australia, where hope and uncertainty meet again. Through quiet struggles, faith, and the presence of those who remain, she begins to rediscover her voice—and the place where she belongs.

To stay updated on upcoming releases:

www.AngelTienLe.com